How To Live and Not Die

Opal Crews

True Potential
REACH THE WORLD

All Scripture quotations, unless otherwise noted, are from the King James Version of the Bible.

How to Live and Not Die

Cover and Interior Page design by True Potential, Inc.

ISBN: (paperback): 9781948794411
ISBN: (ebook): 9781948794428
Library of Congress Control Number:

True Potential, Inc.
PO Box 904, Travelers Rest, SC 29690
www.truepotentialmedia.com

Produced and Printed in the United States of America.

Gail

Thanks for being a window to Path with W...

Table of Contents

Love C...

Introduction

I wrote this book to give glory to God for what He has done in my life. I also believe that many who read it will learn how to enter into the finished work of Jesus Christ and receive their healing. Jesus Himself bore our sicknesses and diseases, as well as our sins, and provided redemption for whosoever will believe in His great work. His work was an eternal work done for everyone in the world.

God has revealed His will in the Bible, and I will show you from the scriptures that it is God's will that you be healed. We will see from the scriptures that faith is an act and not just mentally agreeing that God's Word is true. Your part is to find out what Jesus Christ did for you, and then believe and act upon His Word. This requires knowledge of God's Word.

There are no incurables with God. If you want to be saved, delivered and healed, believe God's Word in your heart and act upon it. God's Word is living and life-giving. It is God's Word living in you that will produce "zoe" life (zoe [Greek]: the God quality of life).

In this book, I will share with you my testimony of my miracle healing, and what I did to receive my healing. What God did for me, He wills also to do in and for you. In the following chapters I will share with you many things that the Holy Spirit has taught me on the subject of divine healing. Open your heart now to receive God's Word and will for you.

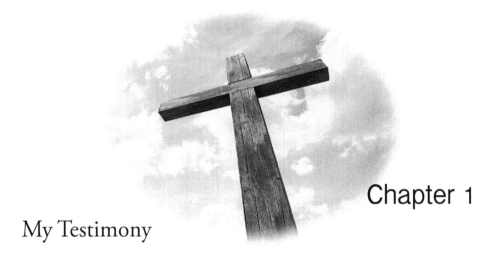

Chapter 1

My Testimony

In the 1970's I began to grow very weak and was experiencing much pain and swelling in many areas of my body. I had difficulty swallowing and little by little my neck began stiffening up until I could no longer turn it. I was diagnosed with crippling arthritis that severely affected my joints. I was also diagnosed with spondylitis, a rare bone disease, which affected my spinal column, fusing my joints together. Later, the orthopedic doctors told me I had a muscle disease and, from all the tests they had run, they were quite sure it was muscular dystrophy. When I received these diagnoses, fear filled me. I believe my fear caused these diseases to progress even more rapidly.

As the spondylitis grew worse, it caused me to be rigid and only able to bend slightly. Over a period of time, the arthritis caused my left hip to become locked and frozen in position. My ankles were stiff, and I limped very badly when I walked. I got to the place where I could no longer walk on uneven ground. I could not walk up and down steps or up the slightest incline without holding on to something or someone.

I knew these diseases were incurable by man and natural medicine. I personally knew about muscular dystrophy because one of my sisters had been bedridden with it for over ten years.

So, having been diagnosed with three incurable diseases, I knew that God was my only hope. I also knew that God still heals today and performs miracles because the Bible says He hasn't changed. Hebrews 13:8 says, *"Jesus Christ the same yesterday, and to day, and for ever."* I had personally experienced His healing power. As a young child, I had been healed of scarlet fever; and as a young adult, I had been healed of hemorrhoids. In 1958 I had been healed of a blood condition and a painful lump on my neck in one of Brother Oral Roberts' meetings.

What I did not know at this time is that Jesus Christ had already obtained healing for us. That it had been bought and paid for in full when He went to the cross and took both our sins and diseases. And when He arose, He ascended into the holy place and offered up His own blood and thereby obtained eternal **redemption** for everyone who would put their trust in Him. (Hebrews 9:12).

Redemption means ransom in full, riddance and Christ's salvation (*Strong's Exhaustive Concordance*).

Yes, I knew God healed, but I did not know how to receive or take my healing by faith. So, over a period of four years, I became a semi-invalid needing almost total care. One of my sisters resigned her job to help with my care. I was perishing for a lack of knowledge (Hosea 4:6).

I knew this was my only answer so I started searching the Bible scriptures on healing and underlining them.

I spent most of my time in bed. Each day I would make myself get up, and sit in a chair to stay as mobile as I could. I would try to sit up for two hours at a time, and then would lie down again; but the pain was constant no matter what I did. As I grew worse, I reached the place where I told my bedfast sister, "I'm not even going to try to get up and sit anymore because it's so difficult." She told me, "Opal, as long as you can put one foot in front of the other, don't stay in bed, because you will get mighty tired of the bed."

Even though we had good health insurance, neither man with all his medical knowledge nor money could buy my health. Therefore, I turned wholeheartedly to the Word of God. I knew this was my only answer so I started searching the Bible scriptures on healing and underlining them. I would read them every day and often several times a day. I prayed to God for my healing. At first, I was trying to talk God into healing me because I did not understand that He had already provided healing for me in Jesus' work on the cross at

Calvary.

You may be starting from that place of not knowing that God heals or not knowing His will in the matter of healing for you, but you too can learn. Praise God! Open your heart and ask the Holy Spirit of God to give you understanding as you read this book and study the scriptures, and He surely will.

Isaiah 53:1 says, *"Who hath believed our report? And to whom is the arm of the LORD revealed?"* In the beginning when I was praying for God to heal me, I did not yet believe His report. I did not believe that He had already healed me.

Isaiah foretold 700 years before Calvary that Jesus healed us.

Isaiah 53:4, 5

> *⁴ Surely he hath borne our griefs, and carried our sorrows: yet we did esteem him stricken, smitten of God, and afflicted.*
>
> *⁵ But he was wounded for our transgressions, he was bruised for our iniquities: the chastisement of our peace was upon him; and with his stripes we are healed.*

The Bible also says that Jesus took our infirmities and bare our sicknesses. Matthew 8:17 says, *"That it might be fulfilled which was spoken by Esaias the prophet, saying, <u>Himself took our infirmities, and bare our sicknesses.</u>"*

Even though I knew these scriptures, they were not revelation to me. They were not yet real to me. I still lacked understanding of how to take hold of these truths as mine.

Once, when my brother came to visit me, I didn't feel like visiting with him because I had so much pain. I remember saying, "Lord, when are You going to heal me?" I still had hope that He would because He had before, but I did not understand at this time God expected more from me. I had to learn that there is a big difference between hope and faith. Bible hope is earnest expectation, but faith must be added to hope to receive the promises of God and to produce the end result of healing. Hebrews 11:1 says, *"Now faith is the substance of things hoped for, the evidence of **__things not seen__**."* "Things not seen" means not yet revealed to the physical senses.

When I asked the Lord when He was going to heal me, that's when the Holy

Spirit spoke to my spirit and said, "Opal, you're not going to receive your healing this time until you receive it by believing My Word and the work that I have already done for you." Tears filled my eyes as I looked down at my feet that were swelling out over my shoes and I said, "Lord, you're being too hard on me to ask me to believe that you have already healed me with all I feel and see."

This is when the Holy Spirit reminded me of Calvary, how Jesus had gone to the cross and how they had beaten His back. Jesus had given His back to those who beat Him, to the smiters, and His cheeks to those who plucked off His hair (Isaiah 50:6). The Holy Spirit reminded me of how they had mocked Jesus and how they had gathered around as He hung on the cross and said to Him, *"You saved others, but yourself you cannot save. Come down from the cross now and we will believe that you are the Son of God."* (Matthew 27:42)

The Lord reminded me that Jesus could have saved Himself that day, but that He willingly hung there to save you and me. I realized how hard it was on the Father when He sent His Son to this earth to be delivered up for us all, to take our sins, to heal us, and to obtain our freedom. And it was hard on Jesus too. It was then that I repented for saying to the Lord, "You're being too hard on me." Then I prayed, "Lord, let your Word come alive in me to where it's not just words I'm reading." I asked the Holy Spirit to teach me, and that's when the Holy Spirit began to open up the scriptures to me giving me insight and understanding through the weeks and months that followed.

It was soon after that when my spiritual mother in the Lord, Sister Beatrice Stansky, who was a retired missionary, sent two ladies to my house to pray for me. Before they prayed, they sat down and went over the healing scriptures that tell us that God, through Christ, provided healing for everyone. Then they prayed for me. After they prayed, they asked me, "Did you receive your healing?" I didn't answer them, so they asked me again. Still I didn't answer, and they asked me a third time. I looked down at my swollen feet and then back at them and said, "Well, I want to tell the truth." They said to me, "What is the truth? Jesus said in John 17:17, *"Thy word is truth."*

Up until this time I had thought I would be lying if I said I was healed when I didn't look and feel like it. My focus was on the natural in what I saw and felt and not on what God had provided for me. The Lord used these two ladies to cause me to think about how the Word is the truth. God was answering my

8

prayer and bringing His Word alive to me just as I had asked.

Another time, in the nighttime, I had a dream about a lady who was in the church I attended, and had received her healing of arthritis by praying the prayer of faith for herself. In my dream I said to her, "Mary, I believe if you came and prayed for me, I would receive my healing." She answered me in the dream and said, "Opal, I will, but you have the Healer living on the inside of you, too." This was another truth I did not know until the Holy Spirit showed me that when we are born again, Jesus Christ, by the Holy Spirit, comes to live in us (Colossians 1:26, 27).

I had many friends, too numerous to call by name, who loved me and prayed for me and believed God could heal me. But some who prayed did not really believe I was healed and could not believe until they saw it with their own eyes.

After I had gotten to the point where I could no longer drive, a dear friend would come to my house so I could go with her to a Bible study. I felt the presence of the Holy Spirit always in these gatherings, and I knew they believed that God still does miracles. Their love and care for me meant so much. They prayed for me often in these meetings; and I'm sure many of them prayed believing, but I still did not receive my healing because I had to learn that one who is in faith believes they receive **when they pray**; that is, before their eyes see the evidence. Mark 11:24 says, *"Therefore, I say unto you, What things soever ye desire, when ye pray, believe that ye receive them, and ye shall have them."*

I was praying and others were praying for me too, yet I remained sick.

I was the one who was going to have to believe I received. But instead, I was still waiting to see if anything happened or changed in my body before I would believe. This was not "receiving faith," and so I grew worse instead of getting better.

I was praying and others were praying for me too, yet I remained sick. It was God's will to heal me, but I just didn't know how to receive it. I did not know I had to trust in the finished work of Jesus Christ regarding sickness, just as I had trusted in Jesus to be my sin-bearer. I had to take Jesus as my Healer by faith, just as I had at age eleven taken Jesus as my Savior. Prayer alone is not enough to be saved (born again), and it's not enough to be healed. There must be an acceptance or a receiving on the individual's side.

Some people think that if you could get enough people praying or a certain one praying for you, the work would be done; but there were many of the saints and many of my own family members praying for me, wanting me to be well again, and still I remained sick.

Even if 1,000 people prayed for you 24 hours a day, you must still at some point in time believe that you have received what you prayed for and count it as yours, regardless of what your physical senses are saying. You must believe you received your healing before there is any physical change. You must take God at His Word. You must believe His Word is truth (John 17:17). You must believe **HIS** report (Isaiah 53:1) that by Jesus stripes you were healed (1 Peter 2:24).

God has promised us that the process of physical healing will begin the moment we believe we have received as it says in the following scriptures.

Matthew 21:22 *"And all things, whatsoever ye shall ask in prayer, believing, ye shall receive."*

1 John 5:14, 15

> *¹⁴ And this is the confidence that we have in him, that, if we ask any thing according to his will, he heareth us:*

> *¹⁵ And if we know that he hear us, whatsoever we ask, we know that we have the petitions that we desired of him.*

Mark 11:24 *"Therefore I say unto you, What things soever ye desire, when ye pray, believe that ye receive them, and ye shall have them."*

You receive your healing immediately when you ask, but the manifestation of that healing is not always immediate. How could I believe I received when every one of my senses said otherwise? I had to learn what believe and receive means. A good definition for these two words is as follows:

Believe: Trust in, rely upon, commit to, cling to, adhere to.

Receive: Seize, lay hold, accept, take as one's own.

I had to trust in, rely on, and commit to God's Word being my final authority. I had to let God's Word rule and reign in my life. If what I saw, felt, or heard was not in agreement with God's Word, I had to choose to believe what God's Word said about the matter. This is what I had not yet done.

Thank God, I finally came to the place where I understood that even though God so loved the world and sent His son to save the world (John 3:16, 17), I still had to respond to His great love in sending His eternal son Jesus to redeem me from the curse of the law (Galatians 3:13, 14). Jesus gave Himself as a ransom for us (1 Timothy 2:6), but I had to believe and receive what He had done for me, including bearing my sicknesses (Isaiah 53:5).

It is not a question of "Is it God's will to save us?" 1 Timothy 2:4 clearly says, *"God wants all men to be <u>saved</u> and to come to a knowledge of the truth."* The Greek word for "saved" is sozo.

Sozo: "SAFE" To save; i.e., deliver or protect, **heal**, preserve, save (self), do well, and be (make) whole (*Strong's Exhaustive Concordance*).

So, when we see the word "save/saved," it is all inclusive of Christ's total work for mankind's spirit, soul and body. This Greek word appears 120 times in 103 verses in the New Testament. I have included some of these scriptures at the end of this chapter for you to see.

The enemy Satan would often come to me with thoughts of discouragement, trying to get me to give up over that entire period of time. The enemy will always try to get us to give up on the Word of God for he knows that as we come to know the truth and act upon that truth, it means his defeat in our lives. He would say to me, "Remember what the doctors said." Then he would say, "You're not healed. You're going to die." The enemy would remind me how the doctors had said these diseases are progressive and would only get worse. The enemy would say how they would bury me up on the mountain next to my mother. He told me to pick out my best-looking outfit to get buried in and even told me I looked good in pink.

I entertained these thoughts for a long time because I didn't know it was the enemy bringing those thoughts to me. The enemy has many wiles (John 8:44, Ephesians 6:11), and if you listen to him, he will keep you from your God-given inheritance of healing. He will try to get you to look at the symptoms and go back to walking by sight and not by faith. 2 Corinthians 5:7 says, *"For we walk by faith and not by sight."* Our faith must always be in the Word of the living God and in the work of Jesus Christ, our Redeemer.

It was very difficult for me to read the Word of God during this time because it was very painful to hold my Bible, but still I would read the healing scriptures daily. I also got the New Testament on cassette tape and some scripture worship songs, as well as teachings by Rev. Kenneth E. Hagin, who had been raised up from a bedfast state and healed from more than one fatal disease after studying faith and healing in the Bible.

I listened to these teachings throughout the day and night. I had reached the place where I was getting very little sleep because of the pain in my body. But as I listened to this man of God teaching on Bible faith, I knew he was saying what God's Word says for I had read through the New Testament many times and even memorized many of the scriptures.

> When I stood up, that's when she said, "Yes, it's you honey. Come on down and get in the prayer line."

Even though I had read and memorized scriptures, I realized from these teachings that I had a part in receiving my healing; so, I started working on the receiving end. God's Word began to bring hope to me and show me my part in receiving what Jesus had provided for me.

I began by submitting myself to the Word of God and acknowledging His Word is truth. First, I believed God's Word and then I claimed my healing of the arthritis and the spondylitis. I didn't at this time claim the healing for the muscle disease because it was still so big in my mind knowing my sister had suffered so long with it.

During this time a lady evangelist, Vicki Jamison (Peterson) was visiting our area, and I had heard that people were being healed in her meetings so, I went. She would call out healings by a word of knowledge which is one of the spiritual gifts God set in the church (1 Corinthians 12), and many were healed. As I sat in her meeting, she called out, "Someone back there is being healed of a muscle disease." And even though she pointed in my direction, I didn't think it was for me since I didn't feel any different, so I remained in my seat. When someone else stood up, the lady evangelist said, "It's not you honey, but come on down and get in the prayer line." She continued saying this many times and as others stood up one by one, she would tell them, "It's not you honey, but come on down and get in the prayer line."

Finally, I decided to stand up because I thought that it could be me since she continued to point in my direction. When I stood up, that's when she said, "Yes, it's you honey. Come on down and get in the prayer line." There must have been 40 or more in the prayer line for various things she had called out. I thought, "There is no way she is going to be able to pray for all these people." So, right then I made a decision, and I said to the Lord from my heart as I stood there in the line, "Lord, whether anyone else ever prays for me again or not, I'm claiming my healing of this muscle disease tonight. I know that it's your Holy Spirit that performs healing in me, just as it was He that performed the new birth in me, and so I claim my healing now. I count it done."

I didn't do this because of what I saw or how I felt, because I didn't look or feel any different. I did this by faith in God's Word. I knew in my heart I had received my healing even though there was no physical change in my body. But that didn't matter because I had let God's Word settle it for me. In 1 Peter 2:24 Peter declared, *By His stripes ye were healed.* God's Word said it, so I believed it and I received it. I quit trying to figure out how God was going to do it. I just claimed my healing by faith.

When I returned home, I asked my family to remove the special chair with the high back I had been sitting in for support, as well as the chair beside it that I would always use to help me stand up. I then had them bring me a regular chair to sit in. I did this because I counted my healing done; so, I should no longer need any special chairs. A few days later, as I sat in a regular chair going over my healing scriptures and studying the Word, I came to Mark 5 and was reading about the little woman with the issue of blood. When I got to verse 34 it seemed as though the scripture was raised (bolded) off the page. Mark 5:34 says, *And he said unto her, Daughter, thy faith has made thee whole; go in peace; and be whole of thy plague.* The Spirit of the Lord spoke to my spirit, "It is time for you to start acting on your faith and for that which you are believing." So, I considered what I could do to show my faith by action. Then I thought, "I would like to go and visit Sister Stansky," the one who was a spiritual mother to me and had prayed much for me.

I had not been able to drive for about three years, and all the symptoms were still in my body. I didn't feel any different than before. My neck was still locked and frozen so that I couldn't turn my head. To get to Sister Stansky's house, it would require that I cross over a four-lane street; so, I asked my sister Elizabeth, who had been caring for me for a few years now but no longer drove, if she would go with me to make sure traffic was clear for me to cross. She answered back in a very sharp tone, "No! You just wait until you're feeling better." She did not see any outward change in me so she did not believe I was healed. She would not go nor did she want me to go. She wasn't going to believe I was healed until she could see the symptoms gone, but I knew the Lord had said that it was time for me to act on what I had believed.

So, when I finished my devotion time, I got my keys, made my way to my car and asked the Lord to watch over me. I drove to the four-lane street, used my peripheral vision as much as I could, and crossed over and turned to go to my friend's house. When I arrived, I told her what had happened and how the Lord had prompted me to act on my faith. The Holy Spirit spoke out through her in tongues and the interpretation was "this is of me," which greatly encouraged me.

As I acted on the Word, there were times that if I had gone by how I felt, I wouldn't have done anything. Sometimes it seemed I would go backward for a while instead of going forward. The enemy would say, "Remember what the doctors said." But instead, I would remember what God's Word said.

After this, most days I would get in my car and go to a nearby store and walk around for a little while. I still limped very badly. My left hip was still locked in place and my right knee still hurt. The enemy (the devil), who is the discourager, would come to my mind with his lies and say, "You're going to fall right here on the floor." But I would quietly quote Isaiah 41:10 which says, *"Fear thou not; for I am with thee: be not dismayed; for I am thy God: I will strengthen thee; yea, I will help thee; yea, I will uphold thee with the right hand of my righteousness."* And this scripture encouraged me very much.

Before I claimed my healing, my daily routine had been that I would try to sit up in a chair for two hours and then I would lie down for two hours. I also continued to go to the Sunday morning worship service at our church when I could. My son would help me get dressed. I would go in for the service and sit on the back seat where I would have something to pull myself up with so I could stand.

A week or two after I had gone to Sister Stansky's, I went to the Sunday 11:00 A.M. service with symptoms still in my body. I sat on the back seat as I usually did. And at the close of the service, prompted in my spirit, I slowly pulled myself up to stand and then I testified to the congregation, "I have taken my healing by faith in the work of Jesus Christ, just as I took Him as my Savior by faith."

I quoted to the congregation Isaiah 53:5 which says: *"But he was wounded for our transgressions, he was bruised for our iniquities: the chastisement of our peace was upon him; and with his stripes we are healed,"* and Matthew 8:17 which says, *"That it might be fulfilled which was spoken by Esaias the prophet, saying, Himself took our infirmities, and bare our sicknesses,"* and I also quoted 1 Peter 2:24 which says, *"Who his own self bare our sins in his own body on the tree, that we, being dead to sins, should live unto righteousness: by whose stripes ye were healed."*

I told them, "And you will see it with your eyes."

Some believed, but many were just as I once was and did not believe. They watched me slowly limp out that day. I didn't look any different. My body didn't feel any different. I didn't know when I would look or feel different, but I had taken hold of God's living Word, and I knew that He Who is faithful to His Word would perform the work in me. I began claiming God's promises as mine throughout the days and nights that lay ahead. Little by little I began to improve, and eventually my healing was totally manifested. It was several months later when they saw my total healing with their eyes.

My healing had been a process. During these months, my joints became unlocked and free. I could turn my neck and head again. I was able to get up and do the things I used to do. I took over my house-work again, and I no longer needed my sister's help. Praise God! God is faithful! He is faithful to His Word!

The enemy would say, "Remember what the doctors said." But instead, I would remember what God's Word said.

In looking back on those "instantaneous" healings I had received in the past, I realized each time I had counted it done. It had been by faith I had counted it as mine, but I just didn't realize that's what I had done. Every healing I had experienced, whether it was immediate or a process, I had counted the healing as mine by faith in the Word of God before I felt or saw it.

After God raised me up from a bed of sickness, He told me, "Go and speak of My faithfulness to My Word." God had also told me many times by His Spirit through Sister Stansky, "Get full of My Word, open your mouth and I will fill it." I have obeyed and done what God has instructed me to do, and He has been faithful to fill my mouth with His Word.

God also said, through Sister Stansky, by the Spirit that, "Many would be delivered through My Words that you shall speak." God has been faithful to do this. I have seen many take hold of God's Word and receive their healing.

In the chapters that follow, I will teach you what the Holy Spirit has taught me on how to receive what God has already provided for you.

Scripture examples of Sozo:

Sozo: "SAFE" To save; i.e., deliver or protect, **heal**, preserve, save (self), do well, and be (make) whole (*Strong's Exhaustive Concordance*).

Matthew 1:21 *"And she shall bring forth a son, and thou shalt call his name Jesus: for he shall save [sozo] his people from their sins."*

Mark 16:15, 16

> *15 And he said unto them, Go ye into all the world, and preach the gospel to every creature.*
>
> *16 He that believeth and is baptized shall be saved [sozo]; but he that believeth not shall be damned.*

Mark 5:22, 23

> *22 And, behold, there cometh one of the rulers of the synagogue, Jairus by name; and when he saw him, he fell at his feet,*
>
> *23 And besought him greatly, saying, My little daughter lieth at the point of death: I pray thee, come and lay thy hands on her, that she may be healed [sozo]; and she shall live.*

Mark 5:27, 28

> *27 When she had heard of Jesus, came in the press behind, and touched his garment.*
>
> *28 For she said, If I may touch but his clothes, I shall be whole [sozo].*

Mark 6:56

And whithersoever he entered, into villages, or cities, or country, they laid the sick in the streets, and besought him that they might touch if it were but the border of his garment: and as many as touched him were made whole [sozo].

Mark 10:51, 52

51 And Jesus answered and said unto him, What wilt thou that I should do unto thee? The blind man said unto him, Lord, that I might receive my sight.

52 And Jesus said unto him, Go thy way; thy faith hath made thee whole [sozo]. And immediately he received his sight, and followed Jesus in the way.

Luke 7:48-50

48 And he said unto her, Thy sins are forgiven.

49 And they that sat at meat with him began to say within themselves, Who is this that forgiveth sins also?

50 And he said to the woman, Thy faith hath saved [sozo] thee; go in peace.

Luke 8:12 *"Those by the way side are they that hear; then cometh the devil, and taketh away the word out of their hearts, lest they should believe and be saved [sozo]."*

James 5:14, 15

14 Is any sick among you? let him call for the elders of the church; and let them pray over him, anointing him with oil in the name of the Lord:

15 And the prayer of faith shall save [sozo] the sick, and the Lord shall raise him up; and if he have committed sins, they shall be forgiven him.

NOTE: We see in these scriptures that when Jesus used the Greek word "sozo" in the gospels, many times He was making reference to physical healing.

Chapter 2

Jesus Christ is Our Salvation

Jesus came to earth to be our salvation. He bought our freedom before we were ever born. Jesus suffered, bled and died so that we could receive all He did for us. In His work at Calvary, He provided for mankind's total needs: spirit, soul <u>and body</u>. Many people never experience any part of His salvation on the earth because they don't know that they have a part in receiving all that Christ did and all that salvation provides, but He did it for them anyway and desires that they receive it as their own.

What does salvation provide?

Salvation (Soteria [Greek]: Rescue or safety [physical or morally]: Deliver, health, save, saving).

What must we know to experience this salvation?

First, we must realize that the Bible is not just a book, but it is a revelation of Jesus Christ, God's eternal Son, and God's plan of salvation and redemption. Calvary was Jesus Christ's destiny before the foundation of the world.

It is so important that we see this work of salvation as having been done for us personally. We enter into this great salvation by hearing, believing, confessing and acting on what God's Word says about us and what He has already done for us.

Salvation is to be proclaimed as a finished work for <u>whosoever</u> will come and believe and enter into what Jesus Christ has provided. The gospel is all about salvation as Paul tells us in Romans 1:16, *"For I am not ashamed of the gospel of Christ: for it is the power of God unto salvation to everyone that believeth; to the Jew first, and also to the Greek [which is all other nations]."* The gospel believed and acted upon brings salvation.

Isaiah foretold much to us of the coming of the One (Jesus) who would be salvation from generation to generation and unto the end of the earth.

Isaiah 49:6 *"It is a light thing that thou shouldest be my servant to raise up the tribes of Jacob, and to restore the preserved of Israel: I will also give thee for a light to the Gentiles, that thou mayest be my **salvation** unto the end of the earth."*

Isaiah 51:6, 8

> ⁶ *Lift up your eyes to the heavens, and look upon the earth beneath: for the heavens shall vanish away like smoke, and the earth shall wax old like a garment, and they that dwell therein shall die in like manner: but my **salvation** shall be for ever, and my righteousness shall not be abolished.*
>
> ⁸ *But my righteousness shall be for ever, and my **salvation** from generation to generation."*

Isaiah 52:7 *"How beautiful upon the mountains are the feet of him that bringeth good tidings, that publisheth peace; that bringeth good tidings of good, that publisheth **salvation**; that saith unto Zion, Thy God reigneth!"*

Isaiah 52:10 *"The LORD hath made bare his holy arm in the eyes of all the nations; and all the ends of the earth shall see the **salvation** of our God.'*

It was foretold in Isaiah 7:14, *"Therefore the Lord himself shall give you a sign; Behold, a virgin shall conceive, and bear a son, and shall call his name Immanuel."* There are many passages in Isaiah that foretell of the coming of Christ. Then, we see the fulfillment of Christ's birth in the New Testament when the Christ is born of the virgin Mary.

Luke 1:26-33

> ²⁶ *And in the sixth month the angel Gabriel was sent from God unto a city of Galilee, named Nazareth,*
>
> ²⁷ *To a virgin espoused to a man whose name was Joseph, of the house of*

David; and the virgin's name was Mary.

28 And the angel came in unto her, and said, Hail, thou that art highly favoured, the Lord is with thee: blessed art thou among women.

29 And when she saw him, she was troubled at his saying, and cast in her mind what manner of salutation this should be.

30 And the angel said unto her, Fear not, Mary: for thou hast found favour with God.

31 And, behold, thou shalt conceive in thy womb, and bring forth a son, and shalt call his name JESUS.

32 He shall be great, and shall be called the Son of the Highest: and the Lord God shall give unto him the throne of his father David:

33 And he shall reign over the house of Jacob for ever; and of his kingdom there shall be no end."

After His birth, Jesus was taken to the temple to be dedicated. We are told that <u>God's salvation is now in the earth</u>.

Luke 2:22, 25-30

22 And when the days of her purification according to the law of Moses were accomplished, they brought him to Jerusalem, to present him to the Lord;

25 And, behold, there was a man in Jerusalem, whose name was Simeon; and the same man was just and devout, waiting for the consolation of Israel: and the Holy Ghost was upon him.

26 And it was revealed unto him by the Holy Ghost, that he should not see death, before he had seen the Lord's Christ.

27 And he came by the Spirit into the temple: and when the parents brought in the child Jesus, to do for him after the custom of the law,

28 Then took he him up in his arms, and blessed God, and said,

29 Lord, now lettest thou thy servant depart in peace, according to thy word:

*30 <u>For mine eyes have seen thy **salvation**</u>."*

Acts 4:12 "<u>*Neither is there salvation in any other*</u>*: for there is none other name under heaven given among men, whereby we must be saved.*"

For much of my Christian life I was not aware of all that salvation included. When I read the words "saved" and "salvation" in the Bible, I thought it just meant being born again; and since I was already born again, I just kept reading. I did not know how to enter into the fullness of salvation, nor did I know all that salvation includes, and this is true of many believers today.

After the finished work of Calvary, Paul tells us how to enter in.

Romans 10:9, 10, 13

> *9 That if thou shalt confess with thy mouth the Lord Jesus, and shalt believe in thine heart that God hath raised him from the dead, thou shalt be saved.*
>
> *10 For with the heart man believeth unto righteousness; and with the mouth confession is made unto salvation.*
>
> *13 For whosoever shall call upon the name of the Lord shall be saved.*

When you have done verses 9, 10 and 13 of Romans 10, you are saved. Salvation is so much more than being born again and receiving eternal life. Verse 10 tells us how we can partake of His full salvation (Rescue or safety [physical or morally]: Deliver, health, save, saving).

Salvation is not something we partake of only one time, but rather we should partake of it on a regular basis while we are in our earthly race.

Believing and confessing is partaking and precedes possessing.

Believing and confessing is partaking and precedes possessing. If we need healing, we believe and confess Jesus as our Healer. If we need safety, we believe and confess Him as our Safety. If we need deliverance or rescue, we believe and confess Him as our Deliverer, our Rescuer, and so on. Believing and confessing enables us to walk in what salvation provided.

I want to share with you a great testimony of a lady who received her healing after she sat in my class. In this class, I was prompted by the Holy Spirit to teach on the meaning of the word "salvation," and I did so for a little over a year. The events of the story happened as follows.

Treva worked at a local, dry cleaners. She had just finished waiting on a customer when she suddenly realized she couldn't move her legs and that her head felt strange. At that time, Treva's granddaughter's husband came in. He called her employer, and the employer said to call 911. The ambulance came and began their routine procedure on the way to the hospital.

Treva said she began to claim Isaiah 53:4,5 which says:

> *4 Surely he hath borne our griefs, and carried our sorrows: yet we did esteem him stricken, smitten of God, and afflicted.*
>
> *5 But he was wounded for our transgressions, he was bruised for our iniquities: the chastisement of our peace was upon him; and with his stripes we are healed.*

Which points us forward to the cross.

Then she quoted 1 Peter 2:24, *"Who his own self bare our sins in his own body on the tree, that we, being dead to sins, should live unto righteousness: by whose stripes ye were healed."* which points us back to the cross where we received our healing.

She began to pray and say, "Lord, this is not your will that this happen to me," and she bound the devil in Jesus' name away from her body.

After examining her at the hospital, they asked if she had a neurosurgeon, and she said "No." They told her, "You're going to need one." She was sent to a larger hospital in the area and they called on a well-known, leading neurosurgeon to immediately meet her there. They did a CAT scan and it showed an aneurysm about the size of a golf ball in the cerebellum area of her brain. After looking at the CAT scan, the doctor was shaking his head and saying, "It's a miracle. It's a miracle. It's just a miracle." Treva asked him what he was talking about. He said that he saw on the scan the aneurism getting smaller and smaller until it was totally gone.

Treva's husband, son and pastor were now there. The doctor took them back and showed them the CAT scan. They all came back saying, "It's just a miracle." Treva told the doctor that she had prayed on the way to the hospital. He replied, "It worked." He told her if anything ever happens to him, that he sure hoped she was around. Treva later told me that it was what she had learned in class about healing being a part of salvation that helped her to receive her miracle. She said that after she prayed and claimed her healing, she just didn't worry about it, but counted it done. After three days of extensive testing, the doctors told her everything was normal and sent her home.

Treva said she never realized before how crucial it was for Christians to get these truths in their heart concerning what our salvation includes. Many others who had sat in this class told me that this study had meant more to them than anything else they had ever studied before because they now had a greater understanding of their salvation. Not only does salvation include being born again, but it also includes healing. They learned that they had a part in receiving their healing just as they had in receiving the new birth. There were others in the class that received healing for their bodies as well. One received healing of a heart condition, one of ulcers, and another who had been having mini strokes received her healing also. They all received their healing when they realized that healing is a part of Christ's salvation. And one lady even said it made the whole Bible come alive to her. All glory to God for the revelation and healings received.

Accepting Jesus as Your Lord and Savior:

Don't wait another minute to be a partaker of the promises of God. Don't put off until tomorrow what can be yours today.

2 Corinthians 6:1, 2

> *¹ We then, as workers together with him, beseech you also that ye receive not the grace of God in vain.*
>
> *² (For he saith, I have heard thee in a time accepted, and in the day of salvation have I succoured [helped] thee: behold, <u>now is the accepted time; behold, now is the day of salvation.</u>*

Hebrews 2:3 *"<u>How shall we escape, if we neglect so great salvation;</u> which at the first began to be spoken by the Lord, and was confirmed unto us by them that heard him."*

1 Timothy 2:4-6

> *⁴ Who will have <u>all men to be saved,</u> and to come unto the knowledge of the truth.*
>
> *⁵ For there is one God, and one mediator between God and men, the man Christ Jesus;*
>
> *⁶ Who <u>gave himself a ransom for all,</u> to be testified in due time.*

2 Peter 3:9 *"The Lord is not slack concerning his promise, as some men count slackness; but is longsuffering to us-ward, <u>not willing that any should perish,</u> but that all should come to repentance."*

If you have not yet received Jesus Christ as your Savior, I encourage you to do so now. God loves you and sent His Son, Jesus Christ, to save you, but you must personally receive Him as Savior. Pray this prayer and mean it from your heart, and you will be born again. You will pass from spiritual death and will receive eternal life.

"Dear God, I believe you sent Jesus Christ, your Son, to take my sins on the cross and that He died and was raised again as the scripture says. I believe, according to Romans 4:25, that He was delivered up for my offenses and He was raised again to justify me. Your Word tells us in Romans 10:9, 10:

> *9 That if thou shalt confess with thy mouth the Lord Jesus, and shalt believe in thine heart that God hath raised him from the dead, thou shalt be saved.*

> *10 For with the heart man believeth unto righteousness; and with the mouth confession is made unto salvation.*

I believe and accept Jesus as my Savior and Lord. I thank you, dear Lord, for saving me."

Now that you are born again and have become a child of God, keep learning His Word and start partaking of His promises!!

Chapter 3
We Only Walk in the Truths We Know and Apply

You can be born again, be a Christian, and even go to heaven when you die without knowing very much about the Word of God; but you cannot walk victoriously in your God-given inheritance unless you know what He has provided and how to access it. You can't walk in divine health, win spiritual battles or put the enemy to flight without knowing and using the Word of God, which is the most powerful weapon on earth that God has given to His children.

God's Word is an eternal truth. Ignoring or rejecting God's Word kept many of God's children from victory in the Old Covenant (Old Testament); and it still keeps many of God's children from walking in victory today.

Let's look at the contrast between Hosea 4:6 and John 8:31, 32 below, and consider the end result of each.

Hosea 4:6 is still in the Bible and still applies today. It says:

> *My people are destroyed for lack of knowledge: because you have rejected knowledge, I will also reject you from being My priest: seeing you have <u>forgotten</u> the law of your God, I also will forget your children.*

It's not that God's people, at that time, didn't know the truth; it's that they had rejected or forgotten the truths they had heard.

John 8:31, 32

"31 Then said Jesus to those Jews which believed on him, If you continue in my word, then are you my disciples indeed.

32 And you shall <u>know</u> the truth, and the truth shall make you free."

Hosea 4:6 says we are destroyed for a lack of knowledge while John 8:31, 32 says we walk free when we know and apply the truth of God's Word.

The word "know," as used in John 8:32, is defined as to know (absolute), in a great variety of applications, and <u>with much using</u>, be aware of, have knowledge, perceive, be resolved, can speak, be sure, understand (*Strong's Exhaustive Concordance*).

We cannot do what we do not know. We cannot believe, apply or partake of what we do not know. We cannot walk in or live out truths we do not know. Knowing the truths of God's Word and applying them is vital to a victorious life in this world.

In the New Testament, which is our covenant today, we need to know everything that Jesus' work at Calvary obtained so that we can apply these truths and live them out in our life. His work was an eternal work done for everyone who would ever live on this earth.

Romans 4:25 *"Who was delivered for our offences, and was raised again for our justification."*

John 3:14-17

14 And as Moses lifted up the serpent in the wilderness, even so must the Son of man be lifted up:

15 That whosoever believeth in him should not perish, but have eternal life.

16 For God so loved the world, that he gave his only begotten Son, that whosoever believeth in him should not perish, but have everlasting life.

17 For God sent not his Son into the world to condemn the world; but that the world through him might be saved.

Hebrews 9:12 *"Neither by the blood of goats and calves, but by his own blood he entered in once into the holy place, having obtained eternal redemption for us."*

We must come to God by putting faith in the finished work of Jesus on the cross. He is the one who came to redeem us and the one who would have all of mankind to be saved. He is the one who gave Himself as a ransom for us (1 Timothy 2:4-6). This was God's eternal plan being fulfilled for fallen mankind. This was the wisdom of God. When God commands us to preach the Gospel to every creature, He means that we should tell them the "Good News" of this redemption (Romans 3:20-24; Ephesians 1:7; Colossians 1:14; Hebrews 9:12).

The work of Jesus Christ is for the entire world, according to John 3:16. It says, "*whosoever would believe*," but believing in Jesus doesn't automatically mean that we experience all that Christ bought for us. Everything that Christ did had become mine when I was born again, but I did not know this and did not apply these truths. I knew I was born again. I could take you to the place where I accepted Jesus Christ as my Savior. I knew I had received the Holy Ghost baptism. I could take you to the place where I was filled with the Spirit. I thought because I loved the Lord, read His Word, went to church and wanted His will to be done in my life that it would just happen. I didn't know I had become an heir to all that Christ did and that He had made me able to partake as it says in Colossians 1:12, "*Giving thanks unto the Father, which hath made us meet to be partakers of the inheritance of the saints in light.*"

We must come to God by putting faith in the finished work of Jesus on the cross.

I just didn't know how to partake. I didn't know then that I was supposed to learn from God's Word all I had been made an heir of when I received Christ as my Lord, and then I was to apply these truths. When I was born again, I was immediately made an heir to all the blessings in Christ (Ephesians 1:3; 2 Corinthians 1:20). I was put in Christ and by His Word and by His Spirit, He came to dwell in me (John 14:20; Colossians 1:26, 27).

Oh, the riches of our inheritance in Him! No monetary value could be placed upon them. Just as an earthly inheritance will not benefit us if we don't know about it and claim it, this is also true concerning our inheritance through Christ's great eternal work.

Let's look at some scriptures in the Bible that when known and applied will bring many victories in our lives.

In my teachings, I have encouraged everyone I have had the pleasure to instruct to learn and apply the truths found in Colossians 1:9-14.

> *9 For this cause we also, since the day we heard it, do not cease to pray for you, and to desire that ye might be filled with the knowledge of his will in all wisdom and spiritual understanding;*
>
> *10 That ye might walk worthy of the Lord unto all pleasing, being fruitful in every good work, and increasing in the knowledge of God;*
>
> *11 Strengthened with all might, according to his glorious power, unto all patience and longsuffering with joyfulness;*
>
> *12 Giving thanks unto the Father, which hath made us meet to be partakers of the inheritance of the saints in light:*
>
> *13 Who hath delivered us from the power of darkness, and hath translated us into the kingdom of his dear Son:*
>
> *14 In whom we have redemption through his blood, even the forgiveness of sins."*

The Holy Spirit quickened (made alive) these verses to my spirit and wants to bring them alive to you too. He wants us to know and partake of these truths. These all belong to us now to apply, walk in and live out daily.

As I said earlier in this chapter, all of these truths became mine the moment I was born again. I had changed kingdoms and became a part of the kingdom of God; but because I did not know these truths, I could not apply them in my life.

The Christians in the city of Colosse were born again, yet they still didn't have complete knowledge of God's will. They lacked complete understanding of spiritual things. Paul wrote Colossians for the entire church, so what was true for them is true for us today.

In the verses mentioned before in this Chapter, God desires us to:

1. Be filled with the knowledge of His will (Colossians 1:9).
2. Walk out these truths (Colossians 1:10).
3. Be strengthened with all might with His glorious power (Colossians 1:11).
4. Know that we have been made able to partake of the inheritance of the saints, which means to take all His provision as ours (Colossians 1:12).

5. Know we have been delivered from the power of darkness, which is Satan's kingdom, power and dominion, and that we have been translated into the kingdom of His dear son (Colossians 1:13).

6. Know the price of our redemption was that Jesus shed His blood for us for the forgiveness of our sins (Colossians 1:14).

Jesus redeemed us from the curse of the law.

Galatians 3:13, 14

13 Christ hath redeemed us from the curse of the law, being made a curse for us: for it is written, Cursed is every one that hangeth on a tree:

14 That the blessing of Abraham might come on the Gentiles through Jesus Christ; that we might receive the promise of the Spirit through faith.

I did not know that every sickness, named or unnamed, is under the curse and that all sin and sickness had come in the earth at the fall of man and is still running rampant in the earth today. I did not know that I could walk free from the curse, and that I was to walk in the blessings of God. Jesus bought our freedom by taking the curse for us; and I now know, from searching the scriptures and letting God's Word be true, that I am an heir of Christ's total work of redemption and salvation. That means I can partake by faith of these promises and provisions throughout my entire stay on this earth and so can you. We are to be resisting and refusing all that Christ has redeemed us from while we live on this earth (Galatians 3:13, 14; James 4:7; 1 Peter 5:8, 9).

We've been born anew. We've been redeemed. We're in the kingdom of God's dear Son. We've been raised with Him according to Ephesians 2:6. All of the blessings belong to us now according to Ephesians 1:3. We are to rule and reign in Christ Jesus as it says in Romans 5:17. We have a rich inheritance according to Ephesians 1:7. We've been made heirs and able to partake according to Colossians 1:12. We've been delivered from Satan's kingdom, power and dominion according to Colossians 1:13. We can do Ephesians 6:10-18 and be strong now. We can do James 4:7 and submit ourselves to God and resist the devil now. And we can do 1 Peter 5:8, 9 and resist steadfast in the faith now.

By partaking and resisting, and holding fast to our confession of God's Word, we overcome the devil and gain the victory (Hebrews 10:23; 1 John 5:4, 5; Revelation 12:11). To partake of the promises and provisions of God means that you <u>take them as yours.</u>

I am realizing more and more that if we settle for less than our full inheritance, our enemy is sure to keep us out. I see in the Word that God has said "yes" to all His promises in Christ Jesus (2 Corinthians 1:20); and if we don't claim them, <u>we doubt them and do without them.</u> We need to always remember the truth of Colossians 2:15 that the devil is a defeated foe and that Jesus spoiled Him and triumphed over Him for us.

We can live victoriously, and the following scriptures tell us how to do this.

Ephesians 6:10-18:

> *[10] Finally, my brethren, be strong in the Lord, and in the power of his might.*
>
> *[11] Put on the whole armour of God, that ye may be able to stand against the wiles of the devil.*
>
> *[12] For we wrestle not against flesh and blood, but against principalities, against powers, against the rulers of the darkness of this world, against spiritual wickedness in high places.*
>
> *[13] Wherefore take unto you the whole armour of God, that ye may be able to withstand in the evil day, and having done all, to stand.*
>
> *[14] Stand therefore, having your loins girt about with truth, and having on the breastplate of righteousness;*
>
> *[15] And your feet shod with the preparation of the gospel of peace;*
>
> *[16] Above all, taking the shield of faith, wherewith ye shall be able to quench all the fiery darts of the wicked.*
>
> *[17] And take the helmet of salvation, and the sword of the Spirit, which is the word of God:*
>
> *[18] Praying always with all prayer and supplication in the Spirit, and watching thereunto with all perseverance and supplication for all saints.*

In Ephesians 1:17-23, Paul prays that the saints (body of Christ, all those born again) would receive revelation knowledge and would know the following truths:

1. Know the hope of His calling.

2. Know the riches of His inheritance in the saints.

3. Know the exceeding greatness of His power.

4. Know that our spiritual battles today against principalities, powers and wicked spirits that are trying to keep us from our blood-bought victories that Jesus Christ obtained for us are the same ones that Jesus has already dealt with and defeated for us.

You are now in Christ if you are born again. You have been blessed with all spiritual blessings in Christ, and that is why our heavenly Father wants us to have revelation knowledge of these mighty truths because once you know and apply these truths, then you will be prepared to fight each spiritual battle and win.

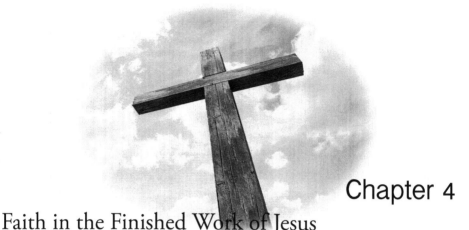

Chapter 4

Faith in the Finished Work of Jesus

I can see in the Word of God that it isn't as much up to God whether mankind will be saved, healed, delivered and walk in victory as it is up to us and our response to the Word of God and the accomplished work of Jesus Christ.

God has told us in His Word that He wills all men to be saved and to come to a knowledge of the truth.

1 Timothy 2:4-6

> *⁴ Who will have all men to be saved, and to come unto the knowledge of the truth.*
>
> *⁵ For there is one God, and one mediator between God and men, the man Christ Jesus;*
>
> *⁶ Who gave himself a ransom for all, to be testified in due time.*

The Bible also says God has already said yes to all His promises (2 Corinthians 1:20). God has told us that once we are born again, we are an heir to all Christ did in His work of redemption. God also tells us that we need a knowledge (revelation) of these things. The Bible says God has given us exceeding great and precious promises.

2 Peter 1:1-4

> *¹ Simon Peter, a servant and an apostle of Jesus Christ, to them that have obtained like precious faith with us through the righteousness of God and*

our Saviour Jesus Christ:

² Grace and peace be multiplied unto you through the <u>knowledge of God</u>, and of Jesus our Lord,

³ According as his divine power hath given unto us all things that pertain unto life and godliness, through the <u>knowledge of him</u> that hath called us to glory and virtue:

⁴ Whereby are given unto us exceeding great and precious promises: that by these ye might be partakers of the divine nature, having escaped the corruption that is in the world through lust.

In these scriptures, the word "knowledge" in the Greek is epignosis and is defined as clear and exact knowledge, expresses a more thorough participation in the object of knowledge and on the part of the subject (person) *(Strong's Exhaustive Concordance).*

In 2 Peter 1:1 the Apostle Peter tells us that we have obtained "like precious faith" just as he and the early saints did. Then in verse 2, Peter tells us that grace and peace will be multiplied to us. How? Through the knowledge of God and of Jesus, our Lord. We see here not only the need for knowledge of God, but also knowledge of what Christ did in His finished work.

Not having knowledge of God or of the work of Christ puts us at a disadvantage.

In 2 Peter 1:3, 4 Peter is telling us that all the promises of God belong to us now. As I was studying these scriptures, I also saw that it is by my partaking or taking these promises as my own that I escape the corruption that is in the world.

Not having knowledge of God or of the work of Christ puts us at a disadvantage. We cannot partake of what we do not know is offered to us. God's Word doesn't work in our lives just because we read the Bible and have head knowledge of what the Word says. It works in our lives when we believe and do what it says. So, we see here that it isn't merely **acquired** knowledge, but **applied** knowledge that brings results in our lives.

Since Calvary, the Holy Spirit performs the Word of God that we believe and act upon in our lives. In the eyes of Father God, the debt has been paid in full for everyone at Calvary. Freedom has been wrought (bought) and is now offered to everyone. This is when our salvation, healing and deliverance was purchased for us.

God has already done something about our every need. Believe it, receive it, accept it, and partake of what Jesus Christ purchased for you. It is all "yes" now according to the Bible.

2 Corinthians 1:19, 20

> *19 For the Son of God, Jesus Christ, who was preached among you by us, even by me and Silvanus and Timotheus, was not yea and nay, but in him was yea.*
>
> *20 For all the promises of God in him are yea, and in him Amen, unto the glory of God by us.*

God has already spoken the Word (John 3:17) and Christ has finished the work (John 4:34). So, what is your reaction going to be? What is your response going to be? Will you believe it? Will you receive it as yours today? God has already spoken concerning your need and He will never violate (change) that which He has spoken (Malachi 3:6).

2 Corinthians 6:1, 2

> *1 We then, as workers together with him, beseech you also that ye receive not the grace of God in vain.*
>
> *2 (For he saith, I have heard thee in a time accepted, and in the day of salvation have I succoured [helped] thee: behold, now is the accepted time; behold, now is the day of salvation.*

Verse 1 says we should *"receive not the grace of God in vain."* How could we receive the grace of God in vain? By not taking advantage of what grace and mercy offers to us today. Grace offers to us, in fact, to the world, everything that Jesus Christ provided for us in His substitutionary work for man's sins and to restore us back to God.

While grace offers it, faith receives it. By grace through faith we are saved. It is a gift of God, not of our works but of Christ's work according to Ephesians 2:8, 9.

Jesus at Calvary bought our freedom. We are simply to believe and act upon what God says He has done for us. Where healing is concerned, if you are waiting to see your manifestation of healing before you believe you are healed, you are missing it. We are to believe because the Word of God says we are healed in Isaiah 53:5, *"But he was wounded for our transgressions, he was bruised for our iniquities: the chastisement of our peace was upon him; and with his stripes we are healed."* The Word of God says Jesus **did heal us** in I Peter 2:24, *"Who his own self bare our sins in his own body on the tree, that we, being dead to sins, should live unto righteousness: by whose stripes ye were healed."* It is our proof, our evidence, while it is still unseen (Hebrews 11:1).

The work has been done. The blood of Jesus is now in the holy place as a witness to the finished work of Jesus. Your believing in the finished work of Jesus and your faith in the Word of God gives the Holy Spirit of God something to perform and manifest in you.

Today it isn't a matter of Jesus healing us. It is a matter of our responding to the work of Christ which He did at Calvary for that is when He did heal us. As we respond in faith, as we believe God's report, the Holy Spirit then begins His work of bringing healing into our bodies by performing the work in us.

It is really up to us now to partake of His promises, to stay built up spiritually by studying and meditating on the Word of God, to apply and do His Word, to guard our tongues, to walk in love, to confess the Word of God, to put away a froward and perverse (contrary) mouth and to stay strong in the Lord and in the power of His might. These things even God Himself can't do for us, but He does instruct us in His Word that we are to do them and that He will help us to do them.

God gave His son, Jesus, Who was delivered up for us all; and in His great work of salvation (healing, deliverance from Satan's kingdom and the forgiveness of sins), eternal life was obtained and is now offered to all who will put their faith in His great work. All of our needs (spirit, soul and body) were met at Calvary through Jesus Christ's finished work.

Chapter 5

Four Vital Steps to Victory

When I became a semi-invalid requiring full-time help, I began a personal study of the Word of God on the subject of healing. In my study, I found the way to victory. One of the accounts in the Bible that helped me so much was the woman with the issue of blood who over 12 years had spent all she had trying to get well, but only grew worse.

Let's look at the steps she took to her victory.

Mark 5:25-27

> *25 And a certain woman, which had an issue of blood twelve years,*
>
> *26 And had suffered many things of many physicians, and had spent all that she had, and was nothing bettered, but rather grew worse,*
>
> *27 When she had heard of Jesus, came in the press behind, and touched his garment.*

In this passage, we see that it doesn't matter how long anyone has been sick or how impossible it seems to be, Jesus still wants you to receive your healing and walk in health.

Verse 25 says this woman had been sick 12 long years. Verse 26 says she had suffered much, spent all she had, but grew worse. Verse 27 says she heard about Jesus and took action: *"When she had heard of Jesus, [she] came in the press behind, and touched his garment."*

Perhaps the one who told the woman about Jesus healing the people was even in the crowd that day (Mark 3:10). We also see the woman believed what she had heard about Jesus the Healer and faith came, just as it says in Romans 10:17, *"So then faith cometh by hearing, and hearing by the word of God."*

In Mark 5:28 the woman began to say what she believed, *"For she said, If I may touch but his clothes, I shall be whole."* In the Amplified version it says, *"For she kept saying, If I only touch His garments, I shall be restored to health."*

The results of her faith are recorded in the following verses:

Mark 5:29-34

> *29 And straightway the fountain of her blood was dried up; and she felt in her body that she was healed of that plague.*

> *30 And Jesus, immediately knowing in himself that virtue had gone out of him, turned him about in the press, and said, Who touched my clothes?*

> *31 And his disciples said unto him, Thou seest the multitude thronging thee, and sayest thou, Who touched me?*

> *32 And he looked round about to see her that had done this thing.*

> *33 But the woman fearing and trembling, knowing what was done in her, came and fell down before him, and told him all the truth.*

> *34 And he said unto her, "Daughter, thy faith hath made thee whole; go in peace, and be whole of thy plague."*

While many people were crowding around Jesus besides this woman, as Mark 5:24 says, *"and much people followed him, and thronged him,"* it was only this one little woman who received what she needed because she acted in faith. Healing became hers, and will become yours the moment you believe and act on your faith.

Now, let's look at the four vital steps she took that brought healing to her.

Step 1: Desire.

Her desire to be well was evident, for she had spent all she had trying to get well.

Step 2: Decision.

She heard that Jesus was healing the people. We must always make the decision to believe that Jesus is the Healer and still heals today and to act upon what we believe. Her decision led her to press her way through the crowd to Jesus to touch Him. Now, you may be thinking, "I have no way of touching Him." The Bible tells us we too can touch Him with our faith.

Hebrews 4:14-16

> [14] *Seeing then that we have a great high priest, that is passed into the heavens, Jesus the Son of God, let us hold fast our profession.*
>
> [15] *For we have not an high priest which cannot be touched with the feeling of our infirmities; but was in all points tempted like as we are, yet without sin.*
>
> [16] *Let us therefore come boldly unto the throne of grace, that we may obtain mercy, and find grace to help in time of need."*

Jesus is now seated at the right hand of the Father having obtained healing for us. All we have to do today to touch Him is to believe in the work He did and claim it as our own.

Step 3: Determination.

A much-needed ingredient for victory in obtaining what Jesus Christ has provided for us is to <u>hold fast and not give up</u>. We must have that I-will-not-accept-defeat attitude, that no-faint attitude, and that I'm-holding-fast-to-my-faith attitude. If you are not willing to press on against the opposition of the enemy or the people around you regardless of what they believe, say or do, you will not reach Step 4.

Step 4: Deliverance.

Healing manifested.

After hearing the Word, the truth (Romans 10:17), she believed what she heard. We see the confession of her faith, with the action of her faith in going to Jesus. We see that she had a point of contact. She had a specific time of release of her faith. This was the time she took (received) the provision as hers.

What did the woman do?

- She said it.

- She acted on it.

- She received it.

- <u>And the last thing was she felt it.</u>

If you are waiting to <u>feel</u> something in the physical realm or if you are waiting to <u>see</u> something change before you "believe" you receive, this is not Bible faith. This is not receiving faith.

Bible faith:

Hebrews 11:1 *"Now faith is the substance of things hoped for, the evidence of things not seen."*

II Corinthians 5:7 *"(For we walk by faith, not by sight:)"*

James 2:17, 26: *"17 Even so faith, if it hath not works, is dead, being alone. 26 For as the body without the spirit is dead, so faith without works is dead also."*

This is how we receive all Jesus Christ has provided for us and wills to do in us. It is our rightful inheritance. You can take these same steps to your victory because Hebrews 13:8 tells us, *"Jesus Christ the same yesterday, and to day, and for ever."* It matters not the duration of the disease. The Healer, Jesus Christ, still heals today.

Jesus is still performing His Word today in who so ever will believe; and if you don't give up, He will perform it in you!

Chapter 6
Enemy's #1 Objective is to Steal God's Word

Satan is after one thing and that is God's Word because it contains his defeat and your victory. When one hears the Word of God, Satan immediately comes to steal the Word (seed) which was sown in you. If we want to walk in the freedom that God has provided, we must know, confess and apply the Word of God. We must become a doer of the Word. If you are not standing on, partaking of, believing in, and doing the Word of God that you have heard, then the enemy has stolen it from you. Jesus tells us in John 8:31, 32, *"31 If ye continue in my word, then are ye my disciples indeed;*

32 And ye shall <u>know</u> the truth, and the truth shall make you free."

You must learn to *"put on the whole armour of God, that ye may be able to stand against the wiles of the devil"* (Ephesians 6:11). You must become wise to the enemy's wiles (2 Corinthians 2:11).

If the enemy can steal the Word, he can render you inoperative against him. If he can steal the Word, he can render you ineffective in the kingdom of God because…

If he can steal the Word, he has stolen your weapon.

Ephesians 6:17 commands us to *"Take the helmet of salvation, and the sword of the Spirit, which is the word of God."*

If he can steal the Word, he has stolen your light.

Psalm 119:105 *"Thy word is a lamp unto my feet, and a light unto my path."*

Psalm 119:130 *"The entrance of thy words giveth light; it giveth understanding unto the simple."*

John 12:46 declares, *"I [Jesus] am come a light into the world, that whosoever believeth on me should not abide in darkness."*

God's Word gives us light.

If he can steal the Word, he has stolen your God-given instructions and what thoroughly equips you.

II Timothy 3:16, 17: *"16 All scripture is given by inspiration of God, and is profitable for doctrine, for reproof, for correction, for instruction in righteousness: 17 That the man of God may be perfect, thoroughly furnished unto all good works."*

If he can steal the Word, he has stolen your deliverance.

Psalm 107:20 *"He sent his word, and healed them, and delivered them from their destructions."*

If he can steal the Word, he has stolen your healing.

Proverbs 4:22 *"For they [my words] are life unto those that find them, and health to all their flesh."*

If he can steal the Word, he has stolen your promises to which God has already said "yes" and "amen".

2 Corinthians 1:20 *"For all the promises of God in him are yea, and in him Amen, unto the glory of God by us."*

II Peter 1:4 *"Whereby are given unto us exceeding great and precious promises: that by these ye might be partakers of the divine nature, having escaped the corruption that is in the world through lust."*

If he can steal the Word, he has stolen your inheritance.

Colossians 1:12 *"Giving thanks unto the Father, which hath made us meet to be partakers of the inheritance of the saints in light."*

The Bible confirms this inheritance.

Acts 26:18 *"To open their eyes, and to turn them from darkness to light, and from the power of Satan unto God, that they may receive forgiveness of sins, and inheritance among them which are sanctified by faith that is in me."*

If he can steal the Word, he has stolen the truth from you.

John 17:17 *"Sanctify them through thy truth: thy word is truth."*

John 8:32 *"And ye shall know the truth, and the truth shall make you free."*

John 14:6 *"Jesus saith unto him, I am the way, the truth, and the life: no man cometh unto the Father, but by me."*

If he can steal the Word, he has stolen your faith.

Romans 10:17 *"So then faith cometh by hearing, and hearing by the word of God."*

If he can steal the Word, he has stolen your seed that would have produced the harvest you need.

Mark 4:14-20

> *[14] The sower soweth the word.*
>
> *[15] And these are they by the way side, where the word is sown; but when they have heard, Satan cometh immediately, and taketh away the word that was sown in their hearts.*
>
> *[16] And these are they likewise which are sown on stony ground; who, when they have heard the word, immediately receive it with gladness;*
>
> *[17] And have no root in themselves, and so endure but for a time: afterward, when affliction or persecution ariseth for the word's sake, immediately they are offended.*
>
> *[18] And these are they which are sown among thorns; such as hear the word,*
>
> *[19] And the cares of this world, and the deceitfulness of riches, and the lusts of other things entering in, choke the word, and it becometh unfruitful.*
>
> *[20] And these are they which are sown on good ground; such as hear the word, and receive it, and bring forth fruit, some thirtyfold, some sixty, and some an hundred.*

1 Peter 1:23 *"Being born again, not of corruptible seed, but of incorruptible, by the word of God, which liveth and abideth for ever."*

Acts 19:20 *"So mightily grew the word of God and prevailed."*

If he can steal the Word, he has stolen your mirror that you are to look into and see yourself as God sees you.

James 1:23 *"For if any be a hearer of the word, and not a doer, he is like unto a man beholding his natural face in a glass."*

II Corinthians 3:18 *"But we all, with open face beholding as in a glass the glory of the Lord, are changed into the same image from glory to glory, even as by the Spirit of the Lord."*

If he can steal the Word, he has stolen that which we are to apply for cleansing.

Ephesians 5:26 *"That he might sanctify and cleanse it with the washing of water by the word."*

John 15:3 *"Now ye are clean through the word which I have spoken unto you."*

If he can steal the Word, he has stolen that which would have built you up and given you your inheritance.

Acts 20:32 *"And now, brethren, I commend you to God, and to the word of his grace, which is able to build you up, and to give you an inheritance among all them which are sanctified."*

If he can steal the Word, he has stolen that by which you are to judge yourself.

John 12:48 *"He that rejecteth me, and receiveth not my words, hath one that judgeth him: the word that I have spoken, the same shall judge him in the last day."*

If he can steal the Word, he has stolen that which gives you life.

Matthew 4:4 says, *"But he answered and said, It is written, Man shall not live by bread alone, but by every word that proceedeth out of the mouth of God."*

Proverbs 3:1, 2 commands us, *"¹ My son, forget not my law; but let thine heart keep my commandments:*

² For length of days, and long life, and peace, shall they add to thee."

Proverbs 4:22 says, *"For they are life unto those that find them, and health to all their flesh."*

Proverbs 13:14 declares, *"The law of the wise is a fountain of life, to depart from the snares of death."*

John 6:63 proclaims, *"It is the spirit that quickeneth; the flesh profiteth nothing: the words that I speak unto you, they are spirit, and they are life."*

God's Word is light and life-giving. Let God's Word live in you because it is your light; and God's Word living in you is what makes you a light to others.

If he can steal the Word, he has stolen your message which is the "Good News" that we are to teach, preach and tell others about.

Matthew 28:19, 20: *"¹⁹ Go ye therefore and teach all nations…*

²⁰ teaching them to observe all things whatsoever I have commanded you."

II Timothy 4:1-4

> *¹ I charge thee therefore before God, and the Lord Jesus Christ, who shall judge the quick and the dead at his appearing and his kingdom;*
>
> *² Preach the word; be instant in season, out of season; reprove, rebuke, exhort with all long suffering and doctrine.*
>
> *³For the time will come when they will not endure sound doctrine; but after their own lusts shall they heap to themselves teachers, having itching ears;*
>
> *⁴ And they shall turn away their ears from the truth, and shall be turned unto fables.*

Proverbs 14:25 tells us, *"A true witness delivereth souls, but a deceitful witness speaketh lies."*

As you look into God's Word, you'll see yourself as strong and not weak, healed and not sick because you'll see that Jesus Christ took your sicknesses in His own body on the tree and obtained healing for you (Galatians 3:13, I Peter 2:24).

We must come to God based on the finished work of Jesus Christ Who came to redeem us and give Himself a ransom for us. Our faith is not based upon what we see in the natural realm, how we feel or even by human reasoning, but our faith is based upon what we see in the Word of God. If we want to live a victorious life, we must learn to live our life reflecting on who we are in the kingdom of God based on the finished work of Jesus Christ.

In Matthew 24:35 Jesus says, *"Heaven and earth shall pass away but my words shall not pass away."*

Since everything else we see around us will pass away, why not build your life upon that which is sure. His Word is "more sure" than the ground you walk upon. Begin to study the Word of God to discover all that God has done for you, and then take His promises and provisions as yours.

Chapter 7

Never Blame God

Some Christians die early and go to heaven because of a lack of knowledge of how to receive their healing. I have heard some say, "I just don't believe God heals everybody." I want to know what scripture they are basing this statement on for the Word of God clearly says that Jesus did take our sins and our diseases when He went to the cross (Isaiah 53:5, 1 Peter 2:24), and that this work was for the world (John 3:17).

Have you ever known someone who did not receive their healing? Did you ever think that if anyone would be healed, surely this dear saint would have been? Perhaps you have desired healing for a family member or a dear friend and prayed earnestly for that person, but still, their healing didn't come; and so, you thought it must not be God's will to heal them.

We've all done this. I was once in that place. It isn't God's fault if we do not receive all He has provided for us. It's just easier to blame God and say it wasn't His will than to admit the failure was on our part. Maybe this person who loved God just didn't know how to enter into all Christ Jesus provided.

In the Garden of Eden, Adam blamed God and Eve, and Eve blamed the serpent. Many people today still blame God for what the devil is doing. They would rather put the blame on God's side than to admit that maybe this person didn't know everything they needed to know.

In Hosea 4:6 God says, *"My people are destroyed for a lack of knowledge...."* In Hosea 11:3 God says of His children, *"They knew not that I had healed them."*

A lack of knowledge still keeps people out of His blessings today. Rejecting God's truth will also keep people out, and forgetting the truths we once knew and walked in will definitely keep you out.

Colossians 1:9-14

⁹ For this cause we also, since the day we heard it, do not cease to pray for you, and to desire that <u>ye might be filled with the knowledge of his will</u> in all wisdom and spiritual understanding;

¹⁰ That ye might walk worthy of the Lord unto all pleasing, being fruitful in every good work, and increasing in the knowledge of God;

¹¹ <u>Strengthened with all might,</u> according to his glorious power, unto all patience and longsuffering with joyfulness;

¹² Giving thanks unto the Father, which hath made us meet to be partakers of the inheritance of the saints in light:

¹³ Who hath delivered us from the power of darkness, and hath translated us into the kingdom of his dear Son:

¹⁴ In whom we have redemption through his blood, even the forgiveness of sins:

Ephesians 1:3, 11, 18-23

³ Blessed be the God and Father of our Lord Jesus Christ, who hath blessed us with all spiritual blessings in heavenly places in Christ:

¹¹ In whom also we have obtained an inheritance, being predestinated according to the purpose of him who worketh all things after the counsel of his own will:

¹⁸ <u>The eyes of your understanding being enlightened;</u> that ye may know what is the hope of his calling, and what the riches of the glory of his inheritance in the saints,

¹⁹ And what is the exceeding greatness of his power to us-ward who believe, according to the working of his mighty power,

²⁰ Which he wrought in Christ, when he raised him from the dead and set him at his own right hand in the heavenly places,

²¹ Far above all principality, and power, and might, and dominion, and every name that is named, not only in this world, but also in that which is to come:

²² And hath put all things under his feet, and gave him to be the head over all things to the church,

²³ Which is his body, the fulness of him that filleth all in all.

God wants us to know our inheritance. I had to learn these truths and many others through studying the Word of God. I had to learn that Jesus had obtained healing for me. I had to learn that healing is a part of salvation and it belongs to all the children of God. I had to learn that I could receive Jesus as my Healer in the same way I received Him as my Savior. It's as simple as saying "God, you are my Savior and right now, by faith, I receive you as my Healer."

I also had to learn that I couldn't wait to feel or see something. I had to receive and take my healing by faith. Those who want to see or feel something in the natural realm or in their body before they will believe they have received will need to study God's Word as I did and learn the truth.

Let God's Word settle it for you. We must learn what salvation includes and walk it out; and we must learn that sickness and disease is a work of the enemy, Satan, and not the work of God. God proved it was His will to save us and heal us when Jesus took <u>all</u> our sins and <u>all</u> our sicknesses and diseases at Calvary. We must always base what we believe on God's holy, eternal and unchangeable Word regardless of what others believe or say.

We don't have to talk God into doing what He has already done and wills to do in us, but we must come to Jesus to receive all He did at Calvary, whether it be the new birth, healing, peace or any part of salvation. Sickness is a curse, but Christ redeemed us from the curse when He took our sicknesses and diseases at Calvary.

Galatians 3:13, 14

¹³ Christ hath redeemed us from the curse of the law, being made a curse for us: for it is written, Cursed is every one that hangeth on a tree:

¹⁴ That the blessing of Abraham might come on the Gentiles through Jesus Christ; that we might receive the promise of the Spirit through faith.

When we are born again, we become heirs to the blessing of healing that Jesus bought for us.

To walk out our healing, we must know the enemy will come and that we cannot be ignorant to his devices. 2 Corinthians 2:11 says, *"Lest Satan should get an advantage of us: for we are not ignorant of his devices."* Jesus Himself identifies the work of the devil in John 10:10 when He declares that *"The thief cometh not, but for to steal, and to kill, and to destroy..."* so if stealing, killing or destroying are occurring in your life, we know the enemy is the author.

Perhaps this dear saint didn't do all they were instructed to do in God's Word when the enemy came. The Apostle Paul in Ephesians 4:27 commands us to *"Not give place to the devil."* Peter tells us in 1 Peter 5:8, 9:

> *8 Be sober, be vigilant; because your adversary the devil, as a roaring lion, walketh about, seeking whom he may devour:*
>
> *9 Whom <u>resist</u> stedfast in the faith, knowing that the same afflictions are accomplished in your brethren that are in the world.*

James tells us in the first half of James 4:7 to *"Submit yourselves therefore to God...."* which is submitting ourselves to the Word of God and acknowledging that His Word is the truth. The last half of this verse says, *"<u>Resist</u> the devil, and he will flee from you."* When under attack, we can either sit down and take it or rise up and resist. When we resist the devil, we must act against his works and whatever he is trying to do. Maybe this dear saint didn't know how to resist the devil and his works.

Resist means to act against, to oppose, to withstand and to keep from *(Strong's Exhaustive Concordance).*

The Word of God tells us how to stand against and to withstand any attack of the enemy.

Ephesians 6:10-18

> *10 Finally, my brethren, be strong in the Lord, and in the power of his might.*
>
> *11 Put on the whole armour of God, that ye may be able to stand against the wiles of the devil.*
>
> *12 For we wrestle not against flesh and blood, but against principalities, against powers, against the rulers of the darkness of this world, against spiritual wickedness in high places.*
>
> *13 Wherefore take unto you the whole armour of God, that ye may be able*

to withstand in the evil day, and having done all, to stand.

14 Stand therefore, having your loins girt about with truth, and having on the breastplate of righteousness;

15 And your feet shod with the preparation of the gospel of peace;

16 Above all, taking the shield of faith, wherewith ye shall be able to quench all the fiery darts of the wicked.

17 And take the helmet of salvation, and the sword of the Spirit, which is the word of God:

18 Praying always with all prayer and supplication in the Spirit, and watching thereunto with all perseverance and supplication for all saints.

You can see in these verses that God has not left us an open prey to the enemy, but He has given us weapons which, when used, will defeat and overcome every attack that Satan can bring. Maybe this dear saint didn't know how to receive from God and then to stand in faith. Can we do something we don't know how to do? No, of course not. Maybe this dear saint didn't know how to *"fight the good fight of faith."* (1 Timothy 6:12).

Revelation 12:11 declares, *"And they overcame him [devil] by the blood of the Lamb, and by the word of their testimony; and they loved not their lives unto the death."* We must trust in and rely on the blood of Jesus which has paid for our sins in full, made us righteous before God and thoroughly defeated the devil. Satan has no legal right in our lives since we have been delivered from his kingdom, and from his power and authority and been made able to partake of the inheritance of the saints, but when we do not resist the enemy, we give him place.

The scripture in John 6:38 tells us that when Jesus came to the earth, He did the will of God. Jesus said, *"I came down from heaven, not to do mine own will, but the will of him that sent me."* In John 4:34 Jesus says, *"My meat is to do the will of him who sent me, and to finish his work."* So, all that Jesus did was the will of God. Taking our sins was the will of God, and He was doing the will of God when he took our infirmities and bore our sicknesses also.

We see in Isaiah 53:1 our part is to believe God's report so His power may be revealed on our behalf. What is God's report? The Prophet Isaiah told us in Isaiah 53:5, *"But he was wounded for our transgressions, he was bruised for our iniquities: the chastisement of our peace was upon him; and with his stripes we are healed."* Then Peter declared this finished work of Jesus in 1 Peter 2:24, *"Who his own self bare our sins in his own body on the tree, that we, being dead to sins, should live unto righteousness: by whose stripes ye were healed."* This is God's report. Maybe this dear saint didn't know or believe God's report. We need to have scripture for all we believe and for all we do. Ephesians 5:17 says, *"Wherefore be ye not unwise, but understanding what the will of the Lord is."*

Do you know anyone who died without receiving Jesus? God's Word clearly tells us that God *"will have all men to be saved and to come unto the knowledge of the truth."* (1 Timothy 2:4-6; John 3:14-17) Also in 2 Peter 3:9 we are told that He's *"not willing that any should perish, but that all should come to repentance."* From these verses, we can clearly see God wants everyone to be saved, but we know that not everyone is saved, so God's will is not always done. We should never measure God's will by what any person experiences, but by the Word of God and by the work of His Son. Jesus bought salvation for every man, but only those who believe and act upon what He did receive eternal life and are saved.

We must realize that Jesus showed us the will of God through His finished work at Calvary. If ever God was going to override man's will, He surely would have done so in the Garden of Eden when Adam and Eve believed a lie from Satan and brought death and a curse upon the earth.

When someone fails to receive their healing, some make such statements as "God allowed it to happen for a reason" or "God was testing them" or "God has everything under control" and so forth. Then some will say that God is sovereign, meaning He will do whatever He wants to do. This is man's doctrine, man's reasoning or religious theory, which, when we build our lives upon it, we're building on sinking sand. God is sovereign, but He has chosen to operate within His written Word. In John 8:31, 32 Jesus said, *"³¹ If ye continue in my word, then are ye my disciples indeed;*

³² And ye shall know the truth, and the truth shall make you free."

Since Calvary, the Holy Spirit moves in our lives to perform that which we believe and act upon.

What about God's faithfulness? God is faithful to His Word and in His Word, He promises healing through the finished work of Jesus Christ, and God will never violate His Word. In Psalm 89:34 God says, *"My covenant will I not break, nor alter the thing that is gone out of my lips."* In Psalm 119:89, 90 it says, *"*89 *For ever, O Lord, thy word is settled in heaven.*

90 *Thy faithfulness is unto all generations: thou hast established the earth, and it abideth."*

A lot of times people will wait until it is too late to develop faith in God's Word. Hope says, "I'll get healed sometime." Heart faith says, "It's mine now."

I read of an incident where a pastor's wife had died of cancer at an early age. Years later a traveling minister who taught the integrity of God's Word and that divine healing was and is provided for everyone in redemption held a meeting at the pastor's church. The pastor told him at the end of the week that he had lifted a cloud off his shoulders about his wife dying of cancer. The Pastor told him that when his wife died, the people were all bewildered about her death and that a death pall had hung over the church. His wife was a holy woman, a great woman of prayer, and in ministry with him. The pastor said he had blamed God for her death. The pastor told the minister his wife always believed she was going to get healed and they both thought that was faith, but because she kept putting it off into the future, the disease took its course. She died saying "I believe God is going to heal me." The pastor realized after hearing the minister's teaching that week that they were not in Bible faith, but hope.

So often, Christians do not take advantage of what belongs to them.

Jesus said that healing is the children's bread in Matthew 15:26. The Apostle Paul tells us in Colossians 1:12 that God has made us an heir of all the work of Christ and made us able to partake of it. So often, Christians do not take advantage of what belongs to them. Either they do not know what belongs to them or they do not know how to act on what belongs to them.

We will not need healing in heaven because there is no sickness in heaven. Healing belongs to us now. We can have it now in this world. Jesus has already purchased healing for our body along with the new birth for our spirit. God laid on Jesus not only the sin, sickness, and disease of us all but also the cause of that sickness and disease. What He bore, we do not need to bear.

God has not forgotten any of the promises or the provisions He has made nor has He forgotten the price that was paid. We have redemption through the blood of Jesus, and by His stripes, we were healed.

II Corinthians 1:19, 20:

> *19 For the Son of God, Jesus Christ, who was preached among you by us, even by me and Silvanus and Timotheus, was not yea and nay, but in him was yea.*
>
> *20 For all the promises of God in him are yea, and in him Amen, unto the glory of God by us.*

God is not saying "no" to what He has already said "yes" to, and He has already said "yes" to all His promises.

You don't have to accept what the devil is trying to do. You can and should rise up and resist him and his work. When you are resisting the enemy, you've got to mean it. You didn't have to know a lot to receive Jesus, and you don't have to know a lot to begin to walk in health or in any of the promises of God. Just start where you are and walk in what you know. When you do and continue to study the Word of God, your faith will grow. Confess the Word of God that you know. At first, it may seem like you're just reciting it, but you will get to the place where your confidence will grow, and it will come out of your heart; and when it does, that's when you will see results.

No one can walk in victory for you, and no one can walk in health for you nor can you walk there for someone else. No one will walk in divine health consistently without developing a faith of their own in the finished work of Jesus Christ, and no one can keep you built up spiritually except you. Acts 20:32 say, *"And now, brethren, I commend you to God, and to the word of his grace, which is able to build you up, and to give you an inheritance among all them which are sanctified."*

Jesus obtained healing for us, and it is His will that we know and walk in all He did for us. No one, not even the devil, can keep you from being strong in the Lord and in the power of His might (Ephesians 6:10) when you consistently feed upon God's Word!

If you have diligently prayed for someone's healing and they didn't receive, it's not that God did not hear your prayer. It's just very hard to hold someone here when they desire to go and be with the Lord or if they have had a glimpse of heaven. In a case like this, when you think of them, remember they are with the Lord.

Chapter 8

Difference Between Hope and Faith

Habakkuk 2:4 *"Behold, his soul which is lifted up is not upright in him: but **the just shall live by his faith.** "*

The Word of God says we are to live by faith, but some people are only in hope. Hope has to do with desire and expectation. Bible hope is an earnest expectation for tomorrow, but faith is when you know that what you hope for, what you desire has been granted to you. The child of God needs both hope and faith, but it is faith that receives and takes hold of the work that Christ has already accomplished for us.

Titus speaks of Jesus' return being the blessed hope in Titus 2:13, *"Looking for that blessed hope, and the glorious appearing of the great God and our Saviour Jesus Christ."* We expect Jesus to come again (future) and this is our blessed hope (future), our expectation (again future). For the Christian to use hope to believe for the things Christ has already obtained and provided for us in His first coming is like those Jewish people who are still looking and hoping for the Messiah to come. We who have received Jesus as Savior and Lord know that He did come and did go to Calvary and did become salvation for all who will put their trust in Him. This is faith, not *hope*, and it is faith that receives and possesses God's promises today. Our part is to believe and partake of what Jesus did at Calvary. Faith is now. If you keep putting off receiving what Christ did in His great substitutionary work for one minute, one day, one week, one year or even one second, this is not Bible faith. This is not receiving faith. Faith is always now according to Hebrews 11:1, *"Now faith is the substance of things hoped for, the evidence of things not seen.”*

Are you in hope or in faith? Ask yourself, "Do I believe God's promise is mine even though I don't yet see it or feel it?" If you can say "yes," then you are in faith. If God's Word says it's yours, and you have believed God's report and accepted it as yours, you will count it as yours. Faith believes God's report.

Until you get to the place of believing the promises and provisions of God are yours now, His promises remain future to you. Until you believe you are saved, until you believe you are healed, until you believe you are delivered, it all remains future to you. Faith will not work for you until it is present tense. It is then when the promises become yours even though you don't see it or feel it. Faith is of the heart. Faith is knowing it's yours because God said so in His Word.

There are many references in the Bible saying we are to live by faith.

Habakkuk 2:4 *"Behold, his soul which is lifted up is not upright in him: but **the just shall live by his faith.**"*

Romans 1:16, 17

> *[16] For I am not ashamed of the gospel of Christ: for it is the power of God unto salvation to every one that believeth; to the Jew first, and also to the Greek.*
>
> *[17] For therein is the righteousness of God revealed from faith to faith: as it is written, **The just shall live by faith.***

Galatians 3:11 *"But that no man is justified by the law in the sight of God, it is evident: for, **The just shall live by faith.**"*

Hebrews 10:38 *"Now **the just shall live by faith:** but if any man draw back, my soul shall have no pleasure in him."*

All of these verses clearly tell us the just shall live by faith. Faith is what brings the promise out of the unseen into the seen realm. In Hebrews 11 we see men and women of past generations who simply heard God speak and believed and acted as though He told them the truth, and we see what their faith obtained. These are men and women no different than you and I who simply heard God's Word, believed and acted upon it.

Not everyone in his or her generation believed God or lived by faith, but those mentioned in Hebrews 11 did, and that's who we want to imitate. God calls these men and women people of faith because they put their faith in action.

In Hebrews 11:6, the scripture tells us that *"without faith it is impossible to please him: for he that cometh to God must believe that he is and that he is a rewarder of them that diligently seek him."* In verse 7 we see a good example of Bible faith:

> *By faith Noah, being warned of God of things <u>not seen as yet</u>, moved with fear, prepared an ark to the saving of his house; by the which he condemned the world, and became* heir of the *righteousness which is by faith.*

In this verse, we see that his faith is based upon the Word of God and not upon what he saw or felt. When this word was given to Noah, it had never rained, but Noah believed God's Word and acted upon His Word; and because he did, he and his family were saved.

Faith judges God faithful to keep His Word no matter how long it takes before we see it in this realm.

We also see in verse 11 that faith does not give up: *"Through faith also Sara herself received strength to conceive seed, and was delivered of a child when she was past age because she judged him faithful who had promised."*

Faith judges God faithful to keep His Word no matter how long it takes before we see it in this realm. Faith always believes. So, when it is true Bible faith, you count it as yours even though there may be a period when the thing desired is still unseen, and the only evidence you have is God's Word. It is faith in God's Word that is giving substance to the thing you desire. There is nothing "more sure" than God's Word. It is the only proof you need because all of His promises are yes and amen and are sure to come to pass when you believe, act on it and don't let go.

Take His promises as yours. If you are born again, they belong to you as surely as if we could hold them in our hands or see them with our physical eyes. God's eternal Word is your proof. It is your evidence that you can hold on to while it is unseen. No matter how many times you hear or read the Word of God, you must still believe and put faith in God's Word before you see it or feel it.

Every promise of God that I have truly believed, taken as mine and have held fast to has always come to pass. It may not have been as quick as I would like, but faith is what brought the promise of God out of the unseen realm into the seen realm and was my evidence while it was still unseen and unfelt.

God's Word must always be the basis of our faith for believing. Faith must be built on the unfailing Word of God. Overcoming faith is always placed in the finished work of Jesus.

Chapter 9

Renewing the Mind (A Necessity of Walking in Victory)

We are spirit beings created in the likeness and image of God (Genesis 1:26). We are a spirit, we have a soul, and we live in a body (1 Thessalonians 5:23). The new birth takes place in the spirit of man, but the soul is not changed when we are born again. That is an ongoing process called saving your soul. In speaking to born-again ones, the Apostle James says in James 1:21: "*Wherefore lay apart all filthiness and superfluity of naughtiness, and receive with meekness the engrafted word, which is able to <u>save your souls</u>.*" To walk in victory and be in health, we must renew our mind with the Word of God.

3 John 1:2-4

> *² Beloved, I wish above all things that thou mayest prosper and <u>be in health</u>, even as thy soul prospereth.*
>
> *³ For I rejoiced greatly, when the brethren came and testified of the truth that is in thee, even as thou walkest in the truth.*
>
> *⁴ I have no greater joy than to hear that my children walk in truth.*

We see in these verses that God desires us to walk in health. We also see that to walk in this truth, we must do something about our soulish area, which requires renewing our mind with the Word of God.

We are dealing with two realms in this Earth, the seen and the unseen. These two realms are also known as the temporal and the eternal, the natural and the supernatural. 2 Corinthians 4:18 says, *"While we look not at the things which are seen, but at the things which are not seen: for the things which are seen are temporal; but the things which are not seen are eternal."* There is a natural realm and a spiritual realm. With the natural eye, we see only the natural world, but our help isn't coming from the natural realm because God moves in the spiritual realm. The spiritual realm is more real and more powerful than things seen. The things of the Spirit supersede the things of the natural.

The unrenewed mind will reason you out of the things of God because it follows the wisdom of this world instead of the wisdom of God, which is the Word of God. The unrenewed mind sides with the sense realm and its logic is based upon human reasoning rather than the Word of God. Health and healing belong to us because of the work of Jesus. So, if you need a miracle, your answer isn't coming from the natural realm but the spiritual realm. Faith in God and in the work of Jesus is what brings God's promises and His provisions out of the unseen realm into the seen realm. We must look at the Word of God, which the Bible says is Spirit and it is life. The Word of God is from the Spirit of God. God's Word reveals that there are two wisdoms: the world's wisdom and God's wisdom.

James 3:13-18

> *13 Who is a wise man and endued with knowledge among you? let him shew out of a good conversation his works with meekness of wisdom.*
>
> *14 But if ye have bitter envying and strife in your hearts, glory not, and lie not against the truth.*
>
> *15 This wisdom descendeth not from above, but is earthly, sensual, devilish.*
>
> *16 For where envying and strife is, there is confusion and every evil work.*
>
> *17 But the wisdom that is from above is first pure, then peaceable, gentle, and easy to be entreated, full of mercy and good fruits, without partiality, and without hypocrisy.*
>
> *18 And the fruit of righteousness is sown in peace of them that make peace."*

I Corinthians 1:30 *"But of him are ye in Christ Jesus, who of God is made unto us wisdom, and righteousness, and sanctification, and redemption."*

There are also two spiritual kingdoms: the kingdom of God, which is the kingdom of light, and the kingdom of Satan, which is the kingdom of darkness. Colossians 1:13 says, *"Who hath delivered us from the power of darkness, and hath translated us into the kingdom of his dear Son."*

God is eternal, and God's Word is eternal:

Psalm 119:89, 90: *"⁸⁹ For ever, O Lord, thy word is settled in heaven.*

⁹⁰ Thy faithfulness is unto all generations: thou hast established the earth, and it abideth."

Isaiah 40:8 *"The grass withereth, the flower fadeth: but the word of our God shall stand for ever."*

Redemption is eternal:

Hebrews 9:12 *"Neither by the blood of goats and calves, but by his own blood he [Jesus] entered in once into the holy place, having obtained eternal redemption for us."*

Ephesians 1:7 *"In whom we have redemption through his blood, the forgiveness of sins, according to the riches of his grace."*

Colossians 1:14 *"In whom we have redemption through his blood, even the forgiveness of sins."*

Redemption is ransom in full, riddance, Christ's Salvation *(Strong's Exhaustive Concordance).*

Faith is required. Faith is of God and of the Spirit. Faith reaches out into the spiritual realm and sees through the eyes of faith those things of the Spirit and lays hold on the things promised by God while still unseen naturally.

Hebrews 11:1, 3, 7

> *¹ Now faith is the substance of things hoped for, the evidence of things not seen.*
>
> *³ Through faith we understand that the worlds were framed by the word of God, so that things which are seen were not made of things which do appear."*
>
> *⁷ By faith Noah, being warned of God of things not seen as yet, moved*

*with fear, prepared an ark to the saving of his house; by the which he con-
demned the world, and became heir of the righteousness which is by faith.*

Noah had no evidence, nothing he could see in the natural; but he knew it
was true because he believed God's Word; and because he believed, he acted
on God's Word. This is faith. Just like there are unseen things (germs, winds,
sound waves, etc.) that are real and we deal with in the natural, the spiritual
realm is just as real. There are things we can't see with the natural eye that are
real, such as powerful ministering spirits (angels), and even now their ears are
attuned to the Word of God.

Hebrews 1:14 *"Are they not all ministering spirits, sent forth to minister for them
who shall be heirs of salvation?"*

Psalm 103:20 *"Bless the LORD, ye his angels, that excel in strength, that do his
commandments, hearkening unto the voice of his word."*

The things of the Spirit are real; God, Jesus, the Holy Spirit, the Word and
angels are real. They are all presently here now; but if you look in the natural and walk by human reasoning, all you will ever see and experience are
the natural things. If you look in the Word and walk in the Spirit, you can
and will see spiritually. We as God's children are meant to know and walk
in the wisdom of God. The Apostle Paul tells us in 1 Corinthians 2:14 that
the natural man doesn't receive the things of the Spirit of God, for they are
foolishness unto him, neither can he know them because they are spiritually
discerned. But in the same chapter, he tells the believers that we are to know
and walk in the wisdom of God, which is the higher wisdom.

Paul tells us in 1 Corinthians 1:18 that the preaching of the cross is to them
that perish foolishness; but unto us which are saved, it is the power of God.
Then Paul says we are to know and to walk in the wisdom of God; that the
carnal mind will never know the wisdom of God.

Paul tells the believers in 1 Corinthians 2:9-13

*⁹ But as it is written, Eye hath not seen, nor ear heard, neither have
entered into the heart of man, the things which God hath prepared for
them that love him.*

*¹⁰ But God hath revealed them unto us by his Spirit: for the Spirit sear-
cheth all things, yea, the deep things of God.*

11 For what man knoweth the things of a man, save the spirit of man which is in him? even so, the things of God knoweth no man, but the Spirit of God.

12 Now we have received, not the spirit of the world, but the Spirit which is of God; that we might know the things that are freely given to us of God.

13 Which things also we speak, not in the words which man's wisdom teacheth, but which the Holy Ghost teacheth; comparing spiritual things with spiritual.

The Epistles, which are the letters written in the New Testament to the church, are the wisdom of God, revealing to us those things which the natural eye and the natural man cannot see or comprehend. Therefore, we, of necessity, must renew our minds with the Word of God to know and to walk in His perfect will.

Romans 12:1, 2

1 I beseech you therefore, brethren, by the mercies of God, that ye present your bodies a living sacrifice, holy, acceptable unto God, which is your reasonable service.

2 And be not conformed to this world: but be ye transformed by the renewing of your mind, that ye may prove what is that good, and acceptable, and perfect, will of God.

We are told here to present ourselves to God for service and not to conform to this world's way of thinking or living, and that we are to be changed by God's Word and His Spirit by the renewing of our mind through His Word that we may prove and demonstrate the will of God in our lives.

Ephesians 4:22-24

22 That ye put off concerning the former conversation the old man, which is corrupt according to the deceitful lusts;

23 And be renewed in the spirit of your mind;

24 And that ye put on the new man, which after God is created in righteousness and true holiness.

Romans 8:5-14

> [5] *For they that are after the flesh do mind the things of the flesh; but they that are after the Spirit the things of the Spirit.*
>
> [6] *For to be carnally minded is death; but to be spiritually minded is life and peace.*
>
> [7] *Because the carnal mind is enmity against God: for it is not subject to the law of God, neither indeed can be.*
>
> [8] *So then they that are in the flesh cannot please God.*
>
> [9] *But ye are not in the flesh, but in the Spirit, if so be that the Spirit of God dwell in you. Now if any man have not the Spirit of Christ, he is none of his.*
>
> [10] *And if Christ be in you, the body is dead because of sin; but the Spirit is life because of righteousness.*
>
> [11] *But if the Spirit of him that raised up Jesus from the dead dwell in you, he that raised up Christ from the dead shall also quicken your mortal bodies by his Spirit that dwelleth in you.*
>
> [12] *Therefore, brethren, we are debtors, not to the flesh, to live after the flesh.*
>
> [13] *For if ye live after the flesh, ye shall die: but if ye through the Spirit do mortify the deeds of the body, ye shall live.*
>
> [14] *For as many as are led by the Spirit of God, they are the sons of God.*

Not until you start minding the things of the Spirit will you <u>consistently</u> walk in the things of the Spirit. Spiritual realities are not grasped with the natural or carnal mind.

In this chapter we see two laws, two walks, two mind sets, and actually two responses to God's Word. We also see the Holy Spirit's involvement in bringing victory into our lives.

Romans 8:2, 11, 13, 14, 16, 26-28

> [2] *For the law of the Spirit of life in Christ Jesus hath made me free from the law of sin and death.*
>
> [11] *But if the Spirit of him that raised up Jesus from the dead dwell in you, he that raised up Christ from the dead shall also quicken your mortal*

bodies by his Spirit that dwelleth in you.

[13] For if ye live after the flesh, ye shall die: but if ye through the Spirit do mortify the deeds of the body, ye shall live.

[14] For as many as are led by the Spirit of God, they are the sons of God.

[16] The Spirit itself beareth witness with our spirit that we are the children of God:

[26] Likewise the Spirit also helpeth our infirmities: for we know not what we should pray for as we ought: but the Spirit itself maketh intercession for us with groanings which cannot be uttered.

[27] And he that searcheth the hearts knoweth what is the mind of the Spirit, because he maketh intercession for the saints according to the will of God.

[28] And we know that all things work together for good to them that love God, to them who are the called according to his purpose.

In Romans 8 we see:

- Verse 29: God's Plan,
- Verse 31: God is for us,
- Verse 32: God's supreme gift, His Son,
- Verse 34: Jesus makes intercession for us, and
- Verse 35: Nothing can separate us from God for those who make God's Word and His Spirit their trust.

Yes, the law of the Spirit of life in Christ Jesus has made us free from the law of sin and death (Romans 8:2); but the carnal mind will never know nor walk in the things of the Spirit of God because it sides in with sight, feeling and the wisdom of this world.

It takes renewing the mind with the Word of God to be able to live by faith. While the new birth was instantaneous, the renewing of the mind is an on-going process, and something we should be working on during our entire Christian walk. It involves learning all we have been made an heir to through the work of Jesus Christ. Again, we must renew our mind with the Word of God so we can know and act on what the Word says.

2 Corinthians 10:3-5

³ For though we walk in the flesh, we do not war after the flesh:

⁴ (For the weapons of our warfare are not carnal, but mighty through God to the pulling down of strong holds;)

⁵ Casting down imaginations, and every high thing that exalteth itself against the knowledge of God, and bringing into captivity every thought to the obedience of Christ.

When we are born again, we enter into a new kingdom that is governed by new laws which are found in the Word of God and given by our Heavenly Father, the One Who watches over His Word to perform it.

To know and walk in God's laws will require studying and meditating on God's living Word. It will require humbling yourself, your will, and your way to the Word of God. You must become a doer of the Word, and allow God's Word to live in you and have dominion in your life. We must become Word of God minded. We cannot walk in human reasoning concerning redemption. We must take God at His Word and trust His Word and His work, the work of Jesus Christ in redemption, so that He can perform His Word in us. We must claim our blood-bought inheritance, and partake of Christ's victories and His provision. After the cross, Jesus intended that His redemptive work would be proclaimed as a finished work and an eternal work. Hebrews 9:12 says, *"Neither by the blood of goats and calves, but by his own blood he entered in once into the holy place, having obtained eternal redemption for us."*

Study and meditate much on Colossians 1:9-14. In these verses, we see God wants us to have wisdom of spiritual things so we can walk them out. These verses tell us that He has made us able to partake of the inheritance of the saints in light, that we have already been delivered from Satan's power, control and dominion, that we have been translated into the Kingdom of His Son, and that we have redemption through His blood, even the forgiveness of sins.

Since we are born again, we are in the Kingdom of God and are told that we were made able to partake; therefore, when sickness or any other work of Satan tries to attach itself to us, we are to resist and stand fast in faith in the work of Jesus Christ.

It is not denying that sickness exists; it is denying it any right to have dominion or to exist in our life. The same thing is true about sin. It is not denying that sin exists; it is denying its right to exist in our life. Romans 6:14 says, *"For sin shall not have dominion over you: for ye are not under the law, but under grace."* It is not denying that Satan exists, but denying him any dominion in our life. Jesus did something about Satan, sin and sickness. If Satan, sin and sickness did not exist, Jesus would not have had to go to the cross to redeem us. He redeemed us and broke the power (dominion) of Satan, sin and sickness over our life.

Since Jesus finished His work, we are to refuse (deny) anything from which Jesus has redeemed us to exist or have dominion in our life. Jesus made us an heir to all He did; therefore, our part is to embrace fully that which He has provided and given to us. Natural human reasoning will not do this. The Word of God tells us of Christ's work which was done for the world; and once we accept Jesus, we are to exalt the Word of God and the work of Jesus Christ, our Redeemer, over everything else.

Steps to renewing the mind and walking in it:

1. Find out who you are in Christ and what God has given you by reading and studying the Word of God.

2. Put the Word of God in you by meditating on these scriptures and confessing them as yours.

3. Cast down any wrong thoughts that don't agree with the Word of God and replace them with God's Word.

4. Act on what the Word of God says and not on how you feel.

As you keep the Word of God in your mouth, then you will observe (see) how to do it. And then you will prosper and have success in all you do (Joshua 1:8).

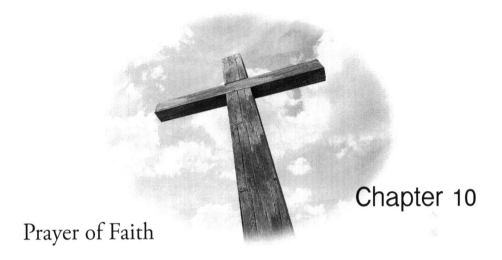

Chapter 10

Prayer of Faith

It is always by grace, through faith that we receive the promises of God. How do we receive?

One way is by praying the prayer of faith. The prayer of faith is a prayer that can be prayed one time as long as when you pray you believe you received. When we pray, we should expect our prayers to be answered. Jesus said in Matthew 21:22 that in *"all things, whatsoever ye shall ask in prayer, **believing**, ye shall **receive.**"* and in Mark 11:24: *"Therefore I say unto you, what things soever ye desire, when ye pray, **believe** that ye **receive** them, and ye shall have them."* The prayer of faith is one that you must believe that you received what you asked for according to God's Word before you see the end result (manifestation).

In these scriptures, Jesus commanded us to believe we have received the things we pray for at the time we pray without waiting until we **see** or **feel** them. It is on this condition that He promises you shall have them. Every time you pray, you believe something. You either believe you receive or you believe you did not receive it as yet. If you believe you did not receive what you prayed for, you are basing your belief on the outward circumstances, physical senses or human reasoning, and not on the Word of God.

Faith is and must always be based on the Word of God, and faith must be released from your heart before the manifestation comes. God's Word instructs us that we release our faith through our words.

Romans 10:8, 10

> *⁸ But what saith it? The word is nigh thee, even in thy mouth, and in thy heart: that is, the word of faith, which we preach;*
>
> *¹⁰ For with the heart man believeth unto righteousness; and with the mouth confession is made unto salvation.*

God's Word also says that faith has action (works).

James 2:14-26

> *¹⁴ What doth it profit, my brethren, though a man say he hath faith, and have not works [corresponding actions]? can faith save him?*
>
> *¹⁵ If a brother or sister be naked, and destitute of daily food,*
>
> *¹⁶ And one of you say unto them, Depart in peace, be ye warmed and filled; notwithstanding ye give them not those things which are needful to the body; what doth it profit?*
>
> *¹⁷ Even so faith, if it hath not works, is dead, being alone.*
>
> *¹⁸ Yea, a man may say, Thou hast faith, and I have works: shew me thy faith without thy works, and I will shew thee my faith by my works.*
>
> *¹⁹ Thou believest that there is one God; thou doest well: the devils also believe, and tremble.*
>
> *²⁰ But wilt thou know, O vain man, that <u>faith without works is dead</u>?*
>
> *²¹ Was not Abraham our father justified by works, when he had offered Isaac his son upon the altar?*
>
> *²² Seest thou how faith wrought with his works, and by works was faith made perfect?*
>
> *²³ And the scripture was fulfilled which saith, Abraham believed God, and it was imputed unto him for righteousness: and he was called the Friend of God.*
>
> *²⁴ Ye see then how that by works a man is justified, and not by faith only.*
>
> *²⁵ Likewise also was not Rahab the harlot justified by works, when she had received the messengers, and had sent them out another way?*
>
> *²⁶ For as the body without the spirit is dead, so faith without works is dead also."*

Many in the church world have no concept of what it means to pray and believe you receive, and then to hold fast to your believing until it comes into manifestation. That's why it's so important for you to get an understanding of the truths in these scriptures so it will benefit you throughout your entire Christian walk.

What is the prayer of faith? Again, it is believing when you prayed that you received what God promised and provided according to 2 Corinthians 1:20, *"For all the promises of God in him are yea, and in him Amen, unto the glory of God by us."* Receiving is always based, not on what I see or how I feel, but on what God says and on what Jesus did. Once I receive by faith, I then hold fast and give thanks and praise to God because I know I have what I asked.

Asking yourself the following questions will help settle it for you and know if you did believe you received when you prayed. Did you believe it was yours? Did you believe that it was granted to you? Did you count it done? If you can answer yes to these questions, you have received what you asked for so hold fast. We are to have confidence that we have received what we asked for.

1 John 5:14, 15

> [14] *And this is the confidence that we have in him, that, if we ask any thing according to his will, he heareth us:*
>
> [15] *And if we know that he hear us, whatsoever we ask, we know that we have the petitions that we desired of him.*

There are other prayers that would be right to pray more than once. The prayer of commitment, which is submitting ourselves, our will and our way to God's purposes and plans for our lives, should be prayed many times. Also, praying for the lost, as Jesus instructed us in Matthew 9:38 to ask the Lord of the harvest to send forth laborers into the field to gather in the harvest, is to be prayed regularly. However, the prayer of faith, which is asking for anything that Jesus has already promised and provided for everyone, only needs to be prayed once <u>if you believed that you received it when you prayed</u>. Just as you pray only once to receive Jesus as Lord, you need only to pray once to receive your healing. From this point on, begin to praise and thank God for your healing.

Find scriptures that cover your need, write them down, read them several times a day, agree with them in your heart, study them, meditate on them, feed on them, and confess (speak) them as yours until your mouth and heart agree. Then do as Hebrews 10:23 says, *"Let us hold fast the profession of our faith without wavering; (for he is faithful that promised;)"* and He will perform it in you.

Once you pray and believe you received and accept your healing, speak your faith and continue to confess, "Lord, I believe that by Your stripes you healed me." The enemy will try to convince you that you are not really believing and not really in faith, especially if the symptoms are still there. Doubt is going to come, especially if you are in a faith fight. You need to know that just because doubt comes to your mind, that does not mean you are doubting in your heart (spirit). If you begin speaking contrary to the Word of God, just stop, repent and ask God to cleanse you and then reposition yourself by getting your heart and mouth agreeing with God again. Go back to what the Word of God says about it; that Jesus did heal you and begin confessing it again continually that it is yours and hold fast.

We don't have to talk God into saving or healing us because they are both part of what Jesus Christ provided on the cross.

When I came to be born again and asked Jesus to be my Lord, that was the time that I believed I received Jesus as my Savior according to Ephesians 2:8. It is the same with healing. When you pray for yourself or someone else prays for you, you must believe at that time that you received it. Isaiah 53:1 says, *"Who hath believed our report and to whom is the arm (power) of the Lord revealed."* Isaiah continues to tell us in Verse 5 that through Christ's work we are healed. 1 Peter 2:24 says that you were healed (this is after Calvary). This is what we are to believe. At some time, you must come to the point that when you pray you believe you have received. You can't wait until the symptoms are gone to believe you received. If you're not there yet, go back and study the healing scriptures and confess them with your mouth until you are sure, and then pray.

We don't have to talk God into saving or healing us because they are both part of what Jesus Christ provided on the cross. When Jesus took our sins and our diseases on the cross, He was showing to the world that it is God's will to save us and heal us. In John 6:38 Jesus says, *"I came down from heaven, not to do my own will, but the will of him that sent me."* We must believe and take the provision as ours by faith, and then hold fast to our believing.

How do we hold fast? By keeping our mouth and heart in agreement with the living Word of God. God not only hears what you are praying, but He also hears what you are saying. After you say "Amen," what do you say then? It is so important what you say after you pray. If you start talking about the problem and speaking unbelief (contrary to the Word of God), you will undo what you just prayed. When you pray, you are submitting yourself to the Word of God and to the authority of His Word. You are believing it, receiving it, and refusing to be moved away from it until it is manifested (performed) in you. If you feel you are wavering (Hebrews 10:23), it's OK to pray it again to reset your course.

The prayer of faith believes that we receive what God has provided no matter what things look like in the natural. God's definition of faith is found in Hebrews 11:1, *"Now faith is the substance of things hoped for, the evidence of things not seen."*

Faith is the assurance, the knowing, and our proof that we have received what we asked of God. As it says in Hebrews 11:1 (AMPC):

> *Now faith is the assurance (the confirmation, the title deed) of the things [we] hope for, being the proof of the things [we] do not see and the conviction of their reality [faith perceiving as real fact what is not revealed to the senses].*

God is faithful to His Word; so, take a fast hold on it and don't let go. Faith comes by hearing and hearing by the Word of God (Romans 10:17) so keep hearing and feeding on the Word!

Chapter 11

What to Do About a Counter Attack

I once heard a statement that a well-known minister of the gospel made. This was a man who was used greatly in the healing ministry. He said people need to know that after they receive their healing, Satan will come with a counter-attack. He said that more Christians lose their healing over a counterattack than any other thing. He said Satan will try to steal your blessing of healing from you by tempting you with a symptom.

This is a truth I wish I had learned much earlier in my life. The enemy, Satan, stole from me my healing two times before I learned what to do, even though God's Word tells us what to do in James 4:7, *"Submit yourselves therefore to God. Resist the devil, and he will flee from you."* When you resist the devil, you are resisting his works.

Resist: To act against, to oppose, to withstand and to keep from (*Strong's Exhaustive Concordance*).

The Apostle Peter also tells us to be on guard and what we are to do.

1 Peter 5:8, 9

> *8 Be sober, be vigilant; because your adversary the devil, as a roaring lion, walketh about, seeking whom he may devour:*
>
> *9 Whom resist stedfast in the faith, knowing that the same afflictions are accomplished in your brethren that are in the world.*

Jesus Himself warns us about the work of our enemy.

John 10:10 *"The thief [the devil] cometh not, but for to steal, to kill, and to destroy: I [Jesus] am come that they might have life, and that they might have it more abundantly."*

Jesus also tells us to hold fast that which you have received.

Revelation 2:25 *"But that which ye have already hold fast till I come."*

Even though I knew that Jesus still heals today, I was not aware that once I had received my healing, I must be on guard concerning Satan, the thief. I want to share with you a time when I lost my healing because I did not know this truth.

After I gave birth to my son, I had hemorrhoids. They were the kind where the swelling takes place inwardly and are very painful. The pain would continue several hours after a bowel movement. The first time I received healing of the hemorrhoids was when my son was about two years old. I attended a revival service at church with the intent of receiving prayer for healing. Before prayer for healing was offered, we all gathered around the altar for a time of prayer. While praying there, the Holy Spirit touched me, and I believed and claimed my healing by faith. When those desiring healing were called, I didn't go up for prayer. After the service was dismissed, one of my family members said to me, "Opal, I thought you were going to be prayed for to receive your healing." I told them that I believed I had already received. I had accepted my healing by faith. My healing was manifested by the next time my bowels moved.

Then the symptoms began to appear again and became as bad as they had been before.

I walked in that healing for a couple of years. Then the symptoms began to appear again and became as bad as they had been before. I thought, "I have lost my healing." I did not know then that I was to resist sickness. The hemorrhoids continued for a few years. I began to pray in my prayer time at home for healing. As I sought the Lord and got in His presence, I received my healing again and walked in it for another few years. But again, I grew lax in my time with the Word of God and with prayer, and the old symptoms came back on me. Again, I thought, "O my, I have lost my healing again."

At this time, I did not know how to resist the devil and his works. I really did not know his works nor did I know how he works. Even though we are told at various times in the scriptures how he works, I did not know that I could or should resist and that I was to act against him and his works. I had thought up until this time that if you love the Lord and want to do what is right and go to church and want God's will done in your life, that it would automatically be done.

Then I came to the time when my life depended on my knowing God's Word personally. It was not that I did not love the Lord and want His will done in my life. I did; but at this time I was perishing because of a lack of knowledge of God's Word and His will and a lack of knowledge of Satan's wiles and his works (Hosea 4:6; Ephesians 6:11; 5:17).

Up until this time I had just been a reader of the Bible, God's Word, not knowing or understanding that I was meant to know these truths and apply them and live them out in my life (John 8:31, 32; 14:15-26; 16:7, 13-15).

So, when the enemy came against me with two incurable bone diseases and an incurable muscle disease, which over a period of time made me a semi-invalid, requiring full-time help, I was not prepared to meet the thief (John 10:10).

I praise God for bringing into my life teachings of the integrity of God's Word that not only could we be healed, but that Jesus Christ did heal us at Calvary! As surely as Jesus Himself took our sins, Jesus Himself bore our sicknesses (Isaiah 53:4, 5; Matthew 8:17; Galatians 3:13, 14; 1 Peter 2:24).

God, our loving heavenly Father, wants us, His children, to walk in health and all that Christ's work provided for us. He wants us to walk free from the curse of sin and sickness, which came at the fall of man. The curse is here in the earth running rampant, but Christ redeemed us from the curse. He took the curse for us and made us an heir of the blessings (Galatians 3:13, 14; 2 Peter 1:1-4; Colossians 1:9-14). Colossians 1:12 says, *"Giving thanks unto the father who has made us meet [able] to be partakers of the inheritance of the saints in light."*

Every sickness is under the curse, whether named or unnamed. Our partaking of the promises and provisions of Christ's work and all that salvation includes is how we escape the corruption that is in the world (2 Peter 1:1-4).

I also learned from the scriptures that the Holy Spirit has come to indwell us (John 16:13, 14), to teach, lead, and guide us into truth, to give us insight and understanding of God's Word and to make the things of God known to us (1 Corinthians 2:9, 10, 12). I had known from my childhood that God could heal the sick. I had been healed several different times of minor ailments. Both of my grandmothers had received miracle healings and some of my aunts as well. But still, I did not know about being on guard against a counterattack. I am most grateful for the gaining of this knowledge.

I have now learned how to fight with the sword of the Spirit, which is the Word of God, the most powerful weapon on earth (Ephesians 6:17; Hebrews 4:12).

This is the same weapon Jesus used when He faced the enemy in Matthew 4:1-11 and Luke 4:1-13. I now walk in health where the hemorrhoids are concerned. The enemy has come with a symptom probably ten to twelve times over the last several years, but I now rise up with the Word of God coming out of my mouth saying, "Oh no! I refuse that. I do not accept that back. I have been redeemed from that illness because that is under the curse, and Christ redeemed me from the curse." One time the battle lasted about five weeks, but I stood fast on the Word of God and would not accept defeat. This happened at a time when I was going to be speaking on healing at a conference. When I returned home from the meeting, the symptoms were all gone.

The enemy has also come back with symptoms of the bone and muscle diseases. Once, several years ago, I had to stand against the attack for a few months, but I knew healing was provided for me by Christ, my Lord. I now knew from God's Word I had been made an heir of all Christ's work. The enemy was defeated again, and I still walk in victory.

Satan has no defense against the Word of God. Keep it in your heart and in your mouth and put the enemy to flight. Do not allow the thief to steal your blood-bought inheritance. God wants His people to get good at resisting those things that Christ has redeemed us from by partaking by faith of all Christ did for us. Hebrews 10:23 says, *Let us hold fast the profession of our faith without wavering; (for he is faithful that promised.)."* We are meant to learn and walk in all the victories Jesus provided for us for our entire stay on this earth.

Chapter 12
God's Roadmap for Walking in Divine Health

God has provided health and healing for us. His will is that we walk in health as well as in all that salvation includes.

Salvation: Rescue or safety (physical or morally): Deliver, health, save, saving (*Strong's Exhaustive Concordance*).

He has given us instructions on how to walk in this salvation in His Word. Even though God's Word tells us He has made provision for our health and healing, each individual has a part to play in walking in what He has provided.

God's old covenant included healing before the cross, and the Bible says we have a new and better covenant than they did so the new covenant certainly includes healing. Hebrews 8:6 says, *"But now hath he [Jesus] obtained a more excellent ministry, by how much also he is the mediator of a better covenant, which was established upon better promises."*

The first covenant God made with the children of Israel was when He brought them out of the land of Egypt, and it was a covenant of healing. The healing covenant is clearly spelled out in the Old Testament.

Exodus 15:26

> *And said, If thou wilt diligently hearken to the voice of the LORD thy God, and wilt do that which is right in his sight, and wilt give ear to his*

commandments, and keep all his statutes, I will put none of these diseases upon thee, which I have brought upon the Egyptians: for I am the LORD that healeth thee.

Exodus 23:25, 26

25 And ye shall serve the LORD your God, and he shall bless thy bread, and thy water; and I will take sickness away from the midst of thee.

26 There shall nothing cast their young, nor be barren, in thy land: the number of thy days I will fulfill.

In Deuteronomy 28:61 God declares that every sickness and every plague is under the curse, and the New Testament declares we have been redeemed from the curse.

Galatians 3:13, 14

13 Christ hath redeemed us from the curse of the law, being made a curse for us: for it is written, Cursed is every one that hangeth on a tree:

14 That the blessing of Abraham might come on the Gentiles through Jesus Christ; that we might receive the promise of the Spirit through faith.

The New Testament is the fulfillment of what the Old Testament prophets pointed to when they foretold of the coming of Christ and the work He would do. Jesus said He fulfilled all that was written of Him in the scriptures.

Luke 24:27 *"And beginning at Moses and all the prophets, he expounded unto them in all the scriptures the things concerning himself."*

Luke 24:44-47

44 And he said unto them, These are the words which I spake unto you, while I was yet with you, that all things must be fulfilled, which were written in the law of Moses, and in the prophets, and in the psalms, concerning me.

45 Then opened he their understanding, that they might understand the scriptures,

46 And said unto them, Thus it is written, and thus it behooved Christ to suffer, and to rise from the dead the third day:

47 And that repentance and remission of sins should be preached in his name among all nations, beginning at Jerusalem.

Matthew 8:17 *"That it might be fulfilled which was spoken by Esaias the prophet, saying, Himself [Jesus] took our infirmities, and bare our sicknesses."*

It's important for you to know that healing has been provided for you by Jesus Christ as it says in the following scriptures:

Isaiah 53:1, 4, 5

> *¹ Who hath believed our report? and to whom is the arm of the Lord revealed?*
>
> *⁴ Surely he [Jesus] hath borne our griefs, and carried our sorrows: yet we did esteem him stricken, smitten of God, and afflicted.*
>
> *⁵ But he was wounded for our transgressions, he was bruised for our iniquities: the chastisement of our peace was upon him; and with his stripes we are healed.*

1 Peter 2:24 *"Who his [Jesus] own self bare our sins in his own body on the tree, that we, being dead to sins, should live unto righteousness: by whose stripes ye were healed."*

Just as those of the old covenant were to hearken diligently to the Word of the Lord spoken by the mouth of the prophets, so are we today. Old covenant believers were to adhere to what the prophets said; and in doing so, could walk free from the curse and receive all the blessings of God. It is just as important now that we hearken diligently to the finished work of Jesus in order to walk in the victories Christ obtained for us.

Jesus' finished work at Calvary provided healing for everyone who would believe. As you read the gospels, you see that Jesus was constantly healing, casting out demons and even raising the dead. So, since Jesus was able to heal during His earthly ministry, this further substantiates that healing was provided before Jesus went to the cross.

The work Jesus did at Calvary was done for the world, which includes everyone that has and would ever live in the earth, including you and me. Jesus died and was raised again to save, heal and deliver us. Jesus did this great work not only so we could go to heaven when we leave here, but He also went to Calvary to provide all that salvation is so that we could live it out in our lives today. God tells us how to obtain this salvation.

Proverbs 4:10, 13: *"¹⁰ Hear, O my son, and receive my sayings; and the years of thy life shall be many."*

"¹³ Take fast hold of instruction; let her not go: keep her; for she is thy life."

The following is a sure way to walk in divine health and a sure cure for any sickness or disease when taken according to directions.

Proverbs 4:20-27

> *²⁰ My son, attend to my words; incline thine ear unto my sayings.* ("Attend" means to give God's Word first place in your life.)
>
> *²¹ Let them not depart from thine eyes; keep them in the midst of thine heart.*
>
> *²² For they are life unto those that find them, and health to all their flesh.*
>
> *²³ Keep thy heart with all diligence; for out of it are the issues of life.*
>
> *²⁴ Put away from thee a froward mouth, and perverse lips put far from thee.* (A froward and perverse mouth is speaking contrary to or opposing what God's Word says.)
>
> *²⁵ Let thine eyes look right on, and let thine eyelids look straight before thee.*
>
> *²⁶ Ponder the path of thy feet, and let all thy ways be established.*
>
> *²⁷ Turn not to the right hand nor to the left: remove thy foot from evil.*

God tells us in this passage that His words are life to those who find them and health to all their flesh. The redeemed are supposed to walk in health. It's important to remember that it is the will of God for you to be healed as the Apostle John says.

3 John 1:2-3 (NKJV)

> *²Beloved, I wish above all things that thou mayest prosper and be in health, even as thy soul prospereth.*
>
> *³For I rejoiced greatly, when the brethren came and testified of the truth that is in thee, even as thou walkest in the truth.*

Find the scriptures that tell you about healing so that you can hold fast to them. Study them, ponder them and speak them to get His Word solidly rooted in your spirit. These are all ways to meditate on the Word as we are instructed to do. Meditate means to ponder, to imagine, mutter, speak, study, talk, utter (*Strong's Exhaustive Concordance*). When you meditate on God's Word, you will come to see the promises as yours.

Some say, even pray, concerning healing "if it is God's will," but God revealed His will through the work of Christ, and that work included healing. The will of God was done through Christ's work at Calvary and the scriptures clearly state that *"Himself took our infirmities,"* (Matthew 8:17) and *"Who his [Jesus] own self bare our sins in his own body on the tree, that we, being dead to sins, should live unto righteousness: by whose stripes ye were healed"* (1 Peter 2:24).

Healing is God's will for you whether you ever receive it or not. Receive means to take, lay hold on, lay claim, seize. His will has been made known through the mouth of the prophets who foretold of the coming of the Redeemer, Jesus Christ, and the work that He would do. When Jesus came, He fulfilled this work when He went to the cross. His salvation is offered to whosoever will believe and receive of His great work which was done for the world.

It is also important to know there is no need to pray for healing and at the same time claim sickness by the words of your mouth; such as talking about your symptoms over and over again. Your words cannot be contrary to what

Healing is God's will for you whether you ever receive it or not.

you pray. They must be in agreement with the Word of God. Proverbs 18:21 makes it clear that, *"Death and life are in the power of the tongue: and they that love it shall eat the fruit thereof."* Proverbs 12:18 says, *"There is that speaketh like the piercings of a sword: but the tongue of the wise is health."* Faith believes "I am healed" rather than "I'm going to be healed." Faith takes healing as one's own. Make sure the words you speak line up with the healing you are believing for no matter what your symptoms are or what doctors, family, friends or anyone else says.

Some people have been taught and believe that everyone has a certain way and a certain time to die. They reference Hebrews 9:27 which says, *"And it is appointed unto men once to die, but after this the judgment."* This is not talking about God choosing a certain day or time for someone to die, but rather it is speaking about we only die one time. Psalm 91:16 says, *"With long life will I satisfy him, and shew him my salvation."*

Our heavenly Father's desire is to get His provision of health into our life, and that is why He tells us how to do so in so many scriptures:

Proverbs 3:1, 2 *"¹ My son, forget not my law; but let thine heart keep my commandments:*

² For length of days, and long life, and peace, shall they add to thee."

Proverbs 9:11 *"For by me thy days shall be multiplied, and the years of thy life shall be increased."*

Psalm 91:14-16

> *¹⁴ Because he [us] hath set his love upon me, therefore will I [God] deliver him: I will set him on high, because he hath known my name.*

> *¹⁵ He shall call upon me, and I will answer him: I will be with him in trouble; I will deliver him, and honour him.*

> *¹⁶ With long life will I satisfy him, and shew him my salvation.*

No one will be able to maintain their healing without developing a faith of their own in God's Holy Word. If symptoms return, you must resist and rebuke every symptom with the Word of God. As you begin to do this, it is important to remember these instructions are from God. The very fact that God's Word tells us it will work this way makes it worth the doing.

God tells us to attend to His Word. This is where it starts for every one of us. When we do this, and we can, we will walk in the provision of healing and health.

Chapter 13
The Natural Realm and the Supernatural Realm

We deal with two realms: natural and supernatural, seen and unseen, temporal and eternal. If you need a miracle, your answer isn't coming from the natural realm; it is coming from the supernatural realm. 2 Corinthians 4:18 says, *"While we look not at the things which are seen, but at the things which are not seen: for the things which are seen are temporal; but the things which are not seen are eternal."*

With the natural eye, we see only the natural realm. With the eye of faith, we can see the supernatural realm. 2 Corinthians 5:7 says, *"For we walk by faith, not by sight" (which means not by the physical senses)."* The things of the Spirit supersede the things of the natural realm. We must learn to look at the Word of God, which is of the Spirit of God. The miracle of healing exists and belongs to us because of the work of Jesus Christ at Calvary and is found in the supernatural realm. The Word of God tells us in Ephesians 1:3, *"Blessed be the God and Father of our Lord Jesus Christ, who hath blessed us with all spiritual blessings in heavenly places in Christ."*

Faith is what brings the promises and provisions of God out of the unseen realm into the seen realm.

Hebrews 11:1, 3, 7

> *¹ Now faith is the substance of things hoped for, the evidence of things not seen.*

³ Through faith we understand that the worlds were framed by the Word of God, so that things which are seen were not made of things which do appear.

⁷ By faith Noah, being warned of God of things not seen as yet, moved with fear, prepared an ark to the saving of his house; by the which he condemned the world, and became heir of the righteousness which is by faith.

God moves in the supernatural realm, which is more real and more powerful than things seen. Faith is of God. It comes from the Word of God. It is received in our spirit and reaches out from our spirit to the spiritual realm and receives from God those things of the spirit. Faith lays hold on the things promised by God while still unseen naturally (2 Corinthians 4:18).

After the Apostle Paul tells us many truths in Ephesians 1, he prays the following.

Ephesians 1:17-23

¹⁷ That the God of our Lord Jesus Christ, the Father of glory, may give unto you the spirit of wisdom and revelation in the knowledge of him:

¹⁸ The eyes of your understanding being enlightened; that ye may know what is the hope of his calling, and what the riches of the glory of his inheritance in the saints,

¹⁹ And what is the exceeding greatness of his power to us-ward who believe, according to the working of his mighty power,

²⁰ Which he wrought in Christ, when he raised him from the dead, and set him at his own right hand in the heavenly places,

²¹ Far above all principality, and power, and might, and dominion, and every name that is named, not only in this world, but also in that which is to come:

²² And hath put all things under his feet, and gave him to be the head over all things to the church,

²³ Which is his body, the fullness of him that filleth all in all.

God wants us to walk in all that is revealed to us in the Book of Ephesians, but we can't do it in the natural. There are things we can't see with the natural eye like the air or the wind, but we can see the effects of them. They exist.

They are real. There are also spiritual things such as angels we can't see with the natural eye, but they are just as real as the air or the wind, and they are powerful. They are ministering spirits as it says in Hebrews 1:14. Psalm 91:11 says, *"For he shall give his angels charge over thee, to keep thee in all thy ways."* Psalm 34:7 says, *"The angel of the LORD encampeth round about them that fear him, and delivereth them."* Psalm 103:20 says, *"Bless the LORD, ye his angels, that excel in strength, that do his commandments, hearkening unto the voice of his word."* Even now their ears are attuned to our words. We can speak in harmony with God's Word and give them something to act upon, or we can speak contrary to His Word and hinder their ministry in our life.

Satan and his demon spirits are at work in the earth today, but Jesus has already defeated them for us. Colossians 2:15 says, *"Having spoiled principalities and powers he made a show of them openly triumphing over them in it."* 1 John 3:8 says, *"For this purpose, the Son of God was manifested, that he might destroy the works of the devil."*

The things of the spirit are real. God is real. Jesus is real. The Word of God is real. The Holy Ghost is real. The angels are real. They are all here now and are ready to help us.

If you are waiting to see something in the natural realm, or if you are waiting to feel something before you believe you receive what Christ Jesus has provided for you, that is not Bible faith, that is not receiving faith. Hebrews 11:1 says, *"Now faith is the substance of things hoped for, the evidence of things not seen."*

Abraham's faith had corresponding action because he did not consider his own body, but believed God.

Romans 4:3, 18, 19

> *³For what saith the scripture? Abraham believed God, and it was counted unto him for righteousness.*
>
> *¹⁸ Who against hope believed in hope, that he might become the father of many nations, according to that which was spoken, So shall thy seed be.*
>
> *¹⁹ And being not weak in faith, he considered not his own body now dead, when he was about an hundred years old, neither yet the deadness of Sarah's womb.*

The Apostle James calls faith that has no corresponding action "dead faith." James 2:17, 26 says, *"¹⁷Even so faith, if it hath not works, is dead, being alone."*

"²⁶ For as the body without the spirit is dead, so faith without works is dead also." Our part today is to find out what God has promised and what Jesus Christ has provided. We put our faith in His work and act upon it by taking and accepting the provision as ours. We take and partake of His work while it is still unseen and unfelt.

We can't wait until we are symptom-free before we believe we receive our healing or that our needs are met. If we believe that we have received our healing now, we are giving the Spirit of God something to perform in us. When we believe Isaiah 53:5, *"But he was wounded for our transgressions, he was bruised for our iniquities: the chastisement of our peace was upon him; and with his stripes we are healed."* and 1 Peter 2:24, *"Who his own self bare our sins in his own body on the tree, that we, being dead to sins, should live unto righteousness: by whose stripes ye were healed,"* and have accepted it as ours, we are to declare and confess these truths continuously while God, by His Holy Spirit, is performing His work in us.

This is what you did to be born again to receive eternal life. You believed in your heart that Jesus is the Son of God, that He bore your sins on the cross and was raised from the dead, so you confessed Him as your Lord and you were saved. Jesus explained to a religious man what then occurs.

John 3:3-6

> *³ Jesus answered and said unto him, Verily, verily, I say unto thee, Except a man be born again, he cannot see the kingdom of God.*
>
> *⁴ Nicodemus saith unto him, How can a man be born when he is old? can he enter the second time into his mother's womb, and be born?*
>
> *⁵ Jesus answered, Verily, verily, I say unto thee, Except a man be born of water and of the Spirit, he cannot enter into the kingdom of God.*
>
> *⁶ That which is born of the flesh is flesh; and that which is born of the Spirit is spirit."*

It was the Holy Spirit that performed this great work in you when you believed and acted upon the Word of God. This is supernatural and is performed by the Spirit of God.

In like manner, it is the Spirit of God who will perform the work of healing in you. Divine healing is supernatural. It is as supernatural as the new birth and is performed by the same Spirit who is the Almighty Spirit of God.

Romans 8:2 and 11 say:

> *² For the law of the Spirit of life in Christ Jesus hath made me free from the law of sin and death.*
>
> *¹¹ But if the Spirit of him that raised up Jesus from the dead dwell in you, he that raised up Christ from the dead shall also quicken your mortal bodies by his Spirit that dwelleth in you.*

When you were born again, you became an heir of the total work of Jesus Christ, and you were made able to partake of all the promises of God (Colossians 1:12). Being an heir is not enough. You still must claim your inheritance to enjoy the provisions provided for you. Claiming your inheritance, just as you would claim an earthly inheritance, is what will take you in to receive healing for your body.

We must see ourselves healed in the Word of God and by the work of Christ at Calvary before we see it in the natural realm. God's Word is the mirror we must look into.

James 1:23-25

> *²³ For if any be a hearer of the word, and not a doer, he is like unto a man beholding his natural face in a glass:*
>
> *²⁴ For he beholdeth himself, and goeth his way, and straightway forgetteth what manner of man he was.*
>
> *²⁵ But whoso looketh into the perfect law of liberty, and continueth therein, he being not a forgetful hearer, but a doer of the work, this man shall be blessed in his deed.*

We must not look at the things that are seen in the natural but look at God's Word which is eternal. As it says in 2 Corinthians 4:18, *"While we look not at the things which are seen, but at the things which are not seen: for the things which are seen are temporal, but the things which are not seen are eternal."*

What things are eternal? Christ's work of redemption was an eternal work as it says in Hebrews 9:12 so God's Word should be our focus. And Hebrews 11:3

says, *"Through faith, we understand that the worlds were framed by the Word of God, so that things which are seen were not made of things which do appear."*

The same one who created the heavens and the earth is the same one from whom your help comes. It is the Spirit of the Lord that is changing you as you look into God's Word. 2 Corinthians 3:17, 18 says:

> *17 Now the Lord is that Spirit: and where the Spirit of the Lord is, there is liberty.*
>
> *18 But we all, with open face beholding as in a glass the glory of the Lord, are changed into the same image from glory to glory, even as by the Spirit of the Lord.*

Do not wait to see the end result which would be the manifestation of your healing in the sense and seen realm before you believe and accept your healing by faith in Christ's work. You must keep your focus on Jesus and His finished work, which He did for you when He went to the cross and obtained eternal redemption for whosoever will believe.

It is important to know that we are not limited to natural help. We have supernatural help from the Lord, but we must access this help by faith.

Chapter 14

How to Receive God's Provision

GOD'S WORD IS THE SEED THAT WILL PRODUCE THE HARVEST YOU NEED

Jesus, the Son of God, teaches us how to get our harvest in order to meet all of our needs. Jesus also tells us why some do not receive their harvest. Jesus tells us that Satan comes to steal the Word or choke it out to keep us from receiving God's provision.

The Bible tells us there are two spiritual kingdoms operating in the earth: the kingdom of God and the kingdom of Satan. God's kingdom is called light and Satan's kingdom is called darkness. Everyone that is born again of the Spirit of God by faith in Christ enters into the kingdom of God.

Jesus says in John 3:3: *"Except a man be born again, he cannot see the kingdom of God."* Then Jesus continues to tell Nicodemus in John 3:5, 6: *"⁵ Except a man be born of water and of the Spirit, he cannot enter into the kingdom of God. ⁶ That which is born of the flesh is flesh; and that which is born of the Spirit is spirit."* This work takes place in our spirit by the Holy Spirit.

Romans 10:9, 10 say:

> *⁹ That if thou shalt confess with thy mouth the Lord Jesus, and shalt believe in thine heart that God hath raised him from the dead, thou shalt be saved.*
>
> *¹⁰ For with the heart man believeth unto righteousness; and with the*

mouth confession is made unto salvation.

If you have done what Romans 10:9, 10 say, then you have been born of the Spirit and you became an heir of everything Christ provided in His death, burial and resurrection. But living out what you have become an heir to isn't automatic. Lack of knowledge, lack of practice or lack of persistence can keep you from your inheritance. In this world, if you had a large inheritance but didn't know about it or how to obtain it, you wouldn't benefit from it. So, it is too in the kingdom of God. We must know what our kingdom benefits are and learn how to obtain them.

God has, through Christ's finished work at Calvary, provided you with a rich inheritance that meets every need you will ever have - spirit, soul and body. Jesus paid the full price for this inheritance. Jesus explains in Mark 4:11 how the kingdom of God works. Jesus calls His Word "seed" that must be received in the heart to produce a harvest. He also exposes our enemy and the wiles he uses to try and steal or choke out the Word from our lives. Jesus teaches us that we who have ears to hear and an open receptive heart to receive His Word can learn how the

God has, through Christ's finished work at Calvary, provided you with a rich inheritance that meets every need you will ever have - spirit, soul and body.

kingdom works. The understanding and revelation of these truths and the doing of them are how I received my healing and is how I continue to receive God's provision to meet all of my needs.

Jesus said it is given to those who are in the kingdom to understand this message, but those that are outside the kingdom cannot understand it. Why can some not understand? Psalm 10:4 says, *"The wicked through the pride of his countenance will not seek after God."* God tells us who the wicked are in Proverbs 10:28 (AMPC): *"The hope of the [uncompromisingly] righteous (the upright, in right standing with God) is gladness, but the expectation of the wicked (those who are out of harmony with God) comes to nothing."* Psalm 119:155 declares, *"Salvation is far from the wicked: for they seek not thy statutes."* God is not in their thoughts.

Jesus tells us in Mark 4:14 that *"The sower sows the Word."* He also tells us in Mark 4:15 that *"And these are they by the way side, where the word is sown; but when they have heard, Satan cometh immediately, and taketh away the word that was sown in their hearts."* The various methods Satan uses to either steal the Word or choke it out to cause it not to produce fruit in our lives is found in the Book of Mark.

Mark 4:16-19

> *[16] And these are they likewise which are sown on stony ground; who, when they have heard the word, immediately receive it with gladness;*
>
> *[17] And have no root in themselves, and so endure but for a time: afterward, when affliction or persecution ariseth for the word's sake, immediately they are offended.*
>
> *[18] And these are they which are sown among thorns; such as hear the word,*
>
> *[19] And the cares of this world, and the deceitfulness of riches, and the lusts of other things entering in, choke the word, and it becometh unfruitful.*

While God's Words are seeds, the enemy's words are also seeds. Proverbs 18:21 declares that *"Death and life are in the power of the tongue [words]; and they that love it shall eat the fruit thereof."* The way we sow God's Word in our hearts is that we see what it says, we see what He [Jesus] has provided, and we take it as ours. We must not be sowing Satan's words in our hearts by thinking about, meditating on, giving attention to or speaking His ways! We must get our focus off the circumstances and onto Jesus and His Word. Those of us who look at Jesus and the work He did for us with a steadfast look will be forgiven, delivered, and healed. Jesus said:

John 3:14-17

> *[14] And as Moses lifted up the serpent in the wilderness, even so must the Son of man be lifted up:*
>
> *[15] That whosoever believeth in him should not perish, but have eternal life.*
>
> *[16] For God so loved the world, that he gave his only begotten Son, that whosoever believeth in him should not perish, but have everlasting life.*
>
> *[17] For God sent not his Son into the world to condemn the world; but that the world through him might be saved.*

Just as the Israelites looked at the serpent on the pole and were saved from death (Numbers 21:6-9), so we must continually look *"unto Jesus the author and finisher of our faith"* (Hebrews 12:2) so we will be saved, delivered, healed and made whole.

Jesus describes the heart soil that is needed to make it all the way to our harvest in Mark 4:20 which says, *"And these are they which are sown on good ground; such as hear the word, and receive it, and bring forth fruit, some thirtyfold, some sixty, and some an hundred."* In my way of thinking, the harvest yield from the seed depends upon the heart soil and the attention we give to the seed because the seed, which is the Word of God, is capable of producing 100-fold every time. So, we see it's those who do not give up on the seed of the Word that receive their harvest.

If you are having trouble letting the Word take root in your heart, follow God's command in Hosea 10:12 to *"break up your fallow ground: for it is time to seek the LORD, till he come and rain righteousness upon you."* The way you break up your fallow ground is to open your heart and receive the Word of God.

How we hear makes the difference between receiving what we need or going away empty. Jesus says in Mark 4:23, *"If anyone has ears to hear, let him hear."* Every man has ears, but not every man makes the decision to hear and take it to heart. So, we can see from this we must make the decision to hear and receive the Word of the Lord. We should receive His Word as God speaking to us personally.

We must also *"take heed what [we] hear,"* according to Mark 4:24. That has to do with the content of what we hear. In Luke 8:18 Jesus warns us to take heed <u>how</u> we hear in the parable of the sower. That has to do with attitude. So, we must always hear His Word and receive His Word with an open, receptive heart.

Continuing in Mark 4:24 Jesus says, *"Unto you that hear shall more be given."* In Mark 4:25 it says, *"For he that hath, to him shall be given and he that hath not [and we could say here he hath not an ear to hear] from him shall be taken even that which he hath."* It is Satan who steals the Word from those who do not hear and those who do not hold fast to it as it says in Mark 4:15. Jesus tells us this is how the kingdom of God works.

Mark 4:26-29

²⁶ So is the kingdom of God, as if a man should cast seed into the ground;

²⁷ And should sleep, and rise night and day, and the seed should spring and grow up, he knoweth not how.

²⁸ For the earth bringeth forth fruit of herself; first the blade, then the ear, after that the full corn in the ear.

²⁹ But when the fruit is brought forth, immediately he putteth in the sickle, because the harvest is come."

We don't have to understand how the seed is going to produce the harvest. We just have to sow the seed in faith and expect a harvest. I didn't understand how God was going to get the spondylitis out of my bones, make my muscles strong again or move the arthritis out of my knees and joints, but I had to quit wondering how He was going to do it. I had to come into a place of complete trust and confidence in the seed. When you stop to consider that the seed is God's Word, then you realize that it is infallible, that it is all-powerful, that it is living, and that it is life-giving.

> You hold on until the healing is complete. Afterward, we must hold fast to the healing Word because even then Satan will come and try to steal our healing.

Patience and confidence in the Word you are sowing in your heart are required according to Mark 4:28, *"For the earth bringeth forth fruit of herself; first the blade, then the ear, after that the full corn in the ear."* You can't give up on the seed if you don't see the full harvest in a night or in a week or in a month. You must keep your confidence and trust in the seed; that is, God's Word that cannot fail. He is faithful to His Word to all generations. Many fail to receive their harvest because they give up too soon on the seed. If I had given up on the Word after a week, a month or a year, I would not have seen my healing come to completion. Healing can come in an instant or it can come progressively over time. How long do you have to hold on to the promise that by Jesus stripes you were healed (already done no matter what symptoms are showing up)? You hold on until the healing is complete. Afterward, we must hold fast to the healing Word because even then Satan will come and try to steal our healing.

Mark 4:29 concludes, *"When the fruit is brought forth, immediately he putteth in the sickle, because the harvest is come."* The harvest would be the full, complete manifestation of what you have been sowing the seed for whether it's healing or whatever it might be. This is how the kingdom of God works.

For much of my life, even though I was a Christian from a young age, I did not understand the message of Mark 4 and Luke 8. I thought if I would just go to church and read my Bible and pray, that would be enough for a life of victory. I thought that God's will would automatically be done in my life. But if you want a harvest of victory over all the works of the enemy, you must sow the seed of God's Word in your heart and tend to it until you get the harvest you need. If you do not get the seed of the Word of God in the soil, which is your heart, and keep it growing there, there will be no harvest that you desire. God and His Word (seed) are one, and He always performs His Word in us when our faith holds fast to it.

Isaiah 55:10, 11

> *10 For as the rain cometh down, and the snow from heaven, and returneth not thither, but watereth the earth, and maketh it bring forth and bud, that it may give seed to the sower, and bread to the eater:*

> *11 So shall my word be that goeth forth out of my mouth: it shall not return unto me void, but it shall accomplish that which I please, and it shall prosper in the thing whereto I sent it.*

The seed doesn't work in one's life until it is received in the heart, the soil. Life is in the seed. The seed doesn't produce lying on a shelf or even because you read it. Allow the seed (God's Word) to get rooted in you for the harvest to be produced. Root out the thorns; any offenses and cares of this life. Sow the seed for the harvest you need. Jesus said the kingdom of God works this way, and it will work in your life if you will but sow the seed with expectation and let it grow and prevail in your life.

The Apostle Paul tells us how the Word of God must be received to be effectual in our lives. In 1 Thessalonians 2:13, after having proclaimed the Word of God to the people, Paul said:

> *For this cause also thank we God without ceasing because when you <u>received the word of God</u> which you <u>heard</u> of us you received it not as the word of men but as it is in truth the word of God which <u>effectually worketh also in you that believe</u>.*

It is not just mentally agreeing that the Word of God is true. It is <u>hearing</u> the Word and again <u>receiving</u> it as God speaking to you. Then <u>believing</u> it and <u>applying</u> it to your life. When it is received in this way, it will produce the harvest that you need. Many people who desperately need a harvest from the promises of God spend no time in His Word sowing the seed into their hearts. Faith comes by hearing and hearing by the Word of God (Romans 10:17). The harvest comes from getting this Word inside of you. God's Word is called the incorruptible seed in 1 Peter 1:23, *"Being born again, not of corruptible seed, but of incorruptible, by the word of God, which liveth and abideth for ever."* God's Word is the seed that changes everything. God's Word sown in your heart will produce the harvest you need for rescue, safety, protection, healing, light, insight, understanding, peace of mind, peace of heart, and deliverance from fear and bondage. Nothing else produces faith and lays hold of the promises except the Word of God.

If you want a harvest of God's Word, you must first open your heart to receive the seed into your heart. Even with a natural seed, if it's not sown, it will never produce a harvest. I like to grow a garden every year, and I always sow the seed of the harvest I desire. I am confident that the seed I plant will produce the crop I want, whether it's a tomato or a pepper. It's sad but many people put more confidence in a natural seed than they do in the living Word of God. Many people don't have a problem with the farmer spending all he has on seed to sow in the soil with great expectation of a harvest. Yet many think it strange that anyone would sow the incorruptible seed of God's Word in their hearts with the expectation of a harvest.

God's Word has not changed. Jesus Christ's work has not changed. Jesus is the same yesterday, today and forever (Hebrews 13:8). God wills to do in us all Christ did for us. If you are a child of God, all of Christ's provision belongs to you now. If you are not yet born again, it is God's will that you be born again into the kingdom of God; and then you too will be an heir of all Christ did. Praise God!

Chapter 15

Living by Faith

God's Word must always be the basis of our faith. We are told in Romans 1:17 that the just shall live by faith.

Romans 1:16 says, *"For I am not ashamed of the gospel of Christ: for it is the power of God unto salvation to every one that believeth."*

Galatians 3:11 says, *"But that no man is justified by the law in the sight of God, it is evident for the just shall live by faith."* This scripture is speaking of the Mosaic law in the Old Testament; but since Christ has come, we are now to live by faith in the finished work that Jesus Christ accomplished for us in redemption.

We cannot live by faith without hearing and receiving the Word of God. Romans 10:17 says, *"So then faith comes by hearing and hearing by the word of God."* The written Word of God is God speaking to us. When the Word of God gets in our heart, our faith will grow.

The number one hindrance to faith is a lack of knowledge of God's Word. Faith begins where the will of God is known (F. F. Bosworth). God reveals His will in His Word. Therefore, we can know His will when we know His Word.

Living by faith is walking in the light of God's Word. If you want to walk and live by faith, you must let God's Word have dominion in your life. God's Word must govern your life. Faith placed in God and His Word is what brings the promises and provisions into our individual lives.

In Hebrews, Chapter 11, we see the results of faith. We see faith in action. We see men and women of past generations who in their generation simply heard God speak, believed, and obeyed what God spoke to them; men and women no different than you and I who simply acted upon God's Word. Everyone in their generation did not believe God nor did they all have faith, but those in Hebrews 11 who chose to believe God are called men and women of faith.

Faith is believing and acting upon God's Word. We see God's definition of faith in Hebrews 11:1, *"Now faith is the substance of things hoped for, the evidence of things not seen."* True Bible faith, according to this scripture, will most often involve a period of time between believing and acting upon God's Word to actually seeing and feeling the end result of our faith. During these times, the Word of God is our only evidence giving substance to the things we desire until they are realized.

In Genesis 17:1-6 God tells Abram to start calling himself Abraham, which means in Hebrew "the father of a great multitude." To do so took great faith because Abram and Sarai, his wife, had no children and, naturally speaking, it was impossible for them to have any. Because Abram believed and obeyed God, he and Sarai had a son in their old age. We are told that we are to walk in the Abraham kind of faith. We will discuss in more detail in a separate chapter how to walk in the faith of Abraham.

Ephesians 2:8, 9 tells us, *"⁸ For by grace are ye saved through faith; and that not of yourselves: it is the gift of God.*

⁹ Not of works, lest any man should boast."

So, it is also by grace (unmerited favor) through faith we enter into all the provisions and blessings Christ obtained for us.

Romans 10:10 says, *"For with the heart man believes unto righteousness; and with the mouth confession is made <u>unto</u> salvation."* Confession of God's Word is vitally important to experiencing this great salvation.

I needed a revelation of the full meaning of salvation (Jesus Christ, the one called Salvation by the prophets) and all that it includes today; i.e. rescue or safety (physical or morally): Deliver, health, save, saving.

Once I learned this truth, I took the healing part as mine by faith just as I had many times claimed the safety part of salvation as mine. I knew I was healed even though many of the symptoms were still in my body.

Faith in God's Word and in Christ's total work is still our entrance into all of God's blessings. As you read the Word of God, find out what Christ did for you in His eternal work. Believe it and take it as yours by faith. We must develop unshakable confidence in the great work Jesus did for us on the cross, and we must claim it as our own. Then the Holy Spirit will perform it in our lives.

Romans 10:10 tells us we are to believe and confess what God says about us in order that it might be done in us. We are to say the same thing that God says. We are to believe and confess before experiencing the end result. Why confession? Because this verse says that confession is made unto salvation. Believe and call yourself what God calls you. This you must do before seeing or feeling that for which you are believing. Hebrews 10:23 says, *"Let us hold fast the profession [confession] of our faith without wavering; (for he [God] is faithful that promised."* How do you hold fast? You never let go of what God has promised.

We must get rid of all unbelief. We must stop thinking and speaking that which is contrary to what God has spoken. We must uproot it, reject it. We must cast down wrong thoughts and doubts. Unbelief does not receive the promises of God. Unbelief is failure to believe and take God at His Word. Taking God at His Word and knowing He is faithful to His Word to all generations comes before the manifestation (Psalm 119:89, 90).

I am so thankful to have learned this truth about salvation and true Bible faith. Galatians 3:13, 14 tells us Christ has redeemed us from the curse of the law and made us an heir of all the blessings through Christ and through faith in His work. Don't claim the curse that you have been redeemed from which is running rampant in the earth today. Also, remember that every sickness is under the curse.

We are told in 1 Peter 5:8, 9

> [8] *Be sober, be vigilant; because your adversary the devil, as a roaring lion, walketh about seeking whom he may devour:*
>
> [9] *Whom resist stedfast in the faith, knowing that the same afflictions are*

accomplished in your brethren that are in the world.

Then James 4:7 says, *"Submit yourselves therefore to God. <u>Resist the devil</u>, and he will flee from you."* So, instead of claiming those things which you have been redeemed from, resist them, and claim what Christ did for you. Hold fast to God's Word. Hold fast to His report. This is serious. This is not a game. This is a fight of faith. Never put more emphasis on the manifestation than you do on God's Holy written Word or on Christ's work on the cross which He did for you. Just keep your trust in God and His Word, and then the manifestation will be forthcoming. The blessing of healing is yours. All that salvation includes is yours.

This is serious. This is not a game. This is a fight of faith.

The total work of Jesus Christ was done for you. Some deny that healing is for us today. When anyone does this, they are actually denying part of the great work Jesus did on the cross for the world. Isaiah 53:5 says, *"But he was wounded for our transgressions, he was bruised for our iniquities: the chastisement of our peace was upon him; and with his stripes we are healed."* Hebrews 13:8 says, *"Jesus Christ is the same yesterday, to day and for ever."* His work has not changed. He still heals today. If we want to walk in all Jesus did, we must put our faith in all He did for us. Romans 4:25 says, *"Who [Jesus] was delivered up for our offences, and was raised again for our justification."* When you act on Hebrews 10:23 and hold fast to your confession without wavering, God will be faithful to perform His work in you.

Your spirit must take hold of God's Word while it is still unseen (Hebrews 11:1). If what you believe for is based on anything other than God's Word, it's not true Bible faith. First, we hear God's Word, then we receive it, and then, through study and meditation on God's Word, our faith grows and then we receive all the promises of God by grace through faith. Why would anyone not want to do God's Word since Jesus tells us in Matthew 24:35, *"Heaven and earth will pass away, but my words shall not pass away."* So, since everything else you see around you will pass away, why not build your life upon that which is sure, upon the Word of the living God? His Word is more sure than the ground you walk upon.

Isaiah prophesied in Isaiah 53:5 that He [Jesus] healed us. Luke 24:44 says:

And he said unto them, These are the words which I spake unto you, while I was yet with you, that all things must be fulfilled, which were written in the law of Moses, and in the prophets, and in the psalms, concerning me.

One day when I was studying Luke 24 and came to this verse, the Holy Spirit reminded me that Jesus Himself said He fulfilled all that had been spoken of Him including Isaiah prophesying that He healed us (Isaiah 53:5). After Jesus had ascended back to the Father, the Apostle Peter tells us in 1 Peter 2:24 that by Jesus stripes we were healed. Isaiah, Jesus, and Peter all spoke for God, so anyone else who speaks the truth cannot but say the same.

To walk by faith, you must understand what faith is; therefore, let's look at Hebrews 11:1 more closely. Hebrews 11:1, *"Now faith is the substance of things hoped for, the evidence of things <u>not seen.</u>"* Note that in the original text "not seen" means not yet revealed to the physical senses.

Faith is not merely mental belief or acceptance that the Word of God is true. "Hope so, think so, maybe so" is not Bible faith. Faith must have both <u>hope</u> (earnest expectation) and <u>evidence</u> (Word of God) before it is seen. The promises and provisions, all the things of God, become yours by faith before they become yours in the seen, sense realm. Both they of the Old Covenant and we of the New Covenant must have God's Word as the basis of our faith. True Bible faith is placing your faith in God's written Word while it is not yet revealed to the physical senses or the seen realm. A good example of this would be Hebrews 11:7 which says:

By faith Noah, being warned of God of <u>things not seen as yet,</u> moved with fear [reverence], prepared an ark to the saving of his house; by the which he condemned the world and became heir of the righteousness which is by faith.

If what you are believing is based on anything other than God's Word, it will not work for you. Be it senses, seeing, feeling, mental assent, human reasoning, even doctrines of men, it is not true Bible faith. Anything short of believing God's Word in your heart and acting upon it is not Bible faith. James 1:22 tells us that it is doing the Word of God that will bring results. Therefore, receiving faith is faith that believes and acts upon God's Word.

Living by faith is being both a hearer and a doer of the written Word of God. It is acting upon the Word that you believe on a daily basis by learning from the scriptures what Christ Jesus did for you and putting faith in it and living it out.

Chapter 16

Agree with God

John 17:17 *"Sanctify them through thy truth: **thy word is truth.**"*

You are not lying when you say what God's Word says about you. So many have thought if they say they're healed when they don't feel healed or look healed, that they would be lying. I've been there myself, but as I studied the scriptures, I found I should believe and say what God says about me and what He did for me. This is faith's way of receiving what He has provided.

From the beginning of time, God declared in Isaiah 46:10, *"the end from the beginning, and from ancient times the things that are not yet done [before it comes to pass]."* Joel 3:10 tells us, *"let the weak say, I am strong."* So, you are not lying when you do this. You're not lying when you say, "I'm healed," even when the symptoms are raging because God's Word declares that in Christ's work, we <u>are</u> healed and <u>were</u> healed.

The basis of faith is believing and confessing God's Word even when you don't see or feel what He has promised. In fact, He tells us in Hebrews 11:1 that *"Faith is the substance of things hoped for, the evidence of things not seen."*

Faith calls things that are not as though they were. We see God did this in the previous passage in Isaiah 46:10. All the prophets did this. Jesus tells **us** to do this (Mark 11:23). Paul said the spirit of faith does this in 2 Corinthians 4:13, *"We **having** the same spirit of faith, according as it is written, I believed, and therefore have I spoken; we also believe, and therefore speak."*

Paul also tells us where faith looks or what faith's focus should be. In 2 Corinthians 4:18 he says, *"While we look not at the things which are seen, but at the things which are not seen: for the things which are seen are temporal; but the things which are not seen are eternal."* God is eternal, God's Word is eternal, and the work of Jesus Christ in redemption is an eternal work (Hebrews 9:12); and this is where we are to look. Hebrews 12:2 tells us Jesus is to be our focus, *"Looking unto Jesus the author and finisher of our faith; who for the joy that was set before him endured the cross, despising the shame, and is set down at the right hand of the throne of God."*

Also, God tells us in Hebrews 10:23 to *"Hold fast the profession of our faith without wavering; (for he is faithful that promised)."* We're to hold fast to our confessions of faith continually. When you are holding fast to something, you don't let go of it. It has to do with you overcoming the enemy who is trying to keep you from your victory according to Revelation 12:11 which says, *"And they overcame him [the devil] by the blood of the Lamb, and by the word of their testimony [confession]; and they loved not their lives unto the death."*

This particular word "confession" or "profession," in the Greek means "saying the same thing." It means to believe and say what God says about our sins, sicknesses and everything else included in salvation. Confession is simply believing with our hearts and repeating with our lips God's own declaration of what we **have** and who we **are** in Christ. God wants to perform in us all that He did in Christ for us.

Calvary bought our freedom. We are simply to believe what God says He has done for us and act upon it. In the following passage, notice that the confession, saying the same thing that God says, is by faith. That is, believing and confessing before experiencing the result.

Romans 10:8-10

> *8 But what saith it? The word is nigh thee, even in thy mouth, and in thy heart: that is, the word of faith, which we preach;*
>
> *9 That if thou shalt confess with thy mouth the Lord Jesus, and shalt believe in thine heart that God hath raised him from the dead, thou shalt be saved.*
>
> *10 For with the heart man believeth unto righteousness; and with the mouth confession is made unto salvation.*

It is confession unto our salvation (Rescue or safety [physical or morally]: Deliver, health, save, saving).

Why confession? It brings salvation. This is God's way, not man's way. What are we to confess? What Christ did for us. How often are we to confess it? Continually, especially when we are in the middle of a battle. In confessing, we are saying what God says about us. This will help us to hold steady during the time of trials. When we are doing Hebrews 10:23, we are holding fast to our confession in the face of all contrary evidence. We take a fast hold on God's Word and we don't let go of our confession of His Word while He is performing it in us. Healing is a process, which begins when you believe and take hold on the Word of God in your heart. You can hinder, even stop the process, with words of doubt or if you don't keep God's Word in your mouth.

Not only are we to say what God says about us, but, at the same time, the Bible is very clear that we are NOT to speak words of unbelief or doubt, such as continually confessing the symptoms. The following verses tell us that we are to agree with and speak the Word of God.

1 Peter 3:10 *"For he that will love life, and see good days, let him refrain his tongue from evil, and his lips that they speak no guile."*

Hebrews 3:12, 19

> *[12] Take heed, brethren, lest there be in any of you an evil heart of unbelief, in departing from the living God.*

> *[19] So we see that they could not enter in because of unbelief.*

Note: This is speaking unbelief, which God calls evil.

Proverbs 4:24 *"Put away from thee a froward mouth, and perverse lips put far from thee."* (froward and perverse or contrary in God's ears).

Psalm 34:11-13

> *[11] Come, ye children, hearken unto me: I will teach you the fear of the LORD.*

> *[12] What man is he that desireth life, and loveth many days, that he may see good?*

> *[13] Keep thy tongue from evil, and thy lips from speaking guile.*

Proverbs 18:21 *"Death and life are in the power of the tongue: and they that love it shall eat the fruit thereof."*

Proverbs 12:18 *"There is that speaketh like the piercings of a sword: but <u>the tongue of the wise is health</u>."*

Christ's work at Calvary and His Word in 1 Peter 2:24 tells us, *"Who his own self bare our sins in his own body on the tree, that we, being dead to sins, should live unto righteousness: by whose stripes ye were healed."* It says you **were** healed, so when you confess, "I am healed," you are really just obeying the Word of the Lord and saying about yourself what God has already said about you in His Word. You are just agreeing with what your Heavenly Father has already declared and provided for you in Christ's work. We are told that we are to believe God's Word, and we are to say what He says about us regardless of what any other person says or believes.

Romans 3:3, 4

> [3] *For what if some did not believe? Shall their unbelief make the faith of God without effect?*
>
> [4] *God forbid: yea, let God be true, but every man a liar; as it is written, That thou mightest be justified in thy sayings, and mightest overcome when thou art judged.*

You are letting God be true and every man a liar who speaks contrary to God's Word as we are instructed to do. In these verses, we see that our believing and saying what God says about us has to do with our being justified in what we are saying and with our overcoming.

When you are confessing God's Word and saying what God says about you, you are taking hold on the Word of God and calling it forth into your life and into this natural seeing realm. We are just declaring what God, in His Word by His prophets, has already declared by the Holy Spirit. One who is in faith believes and agrees and says what God says.

Receiving faith believes God and speaks accordingly. Receiving faith calls things the way that God calls them. Receiving faith believes, speaks and acts upon the Word of God as it says in 2 Corinthians 4:13, *"We having the same spirit of faith, according as it is written, I believed, and therefore have I spoken; we also believe, and therefore speak."*

Some will say when you call yourself "the healed" while symptoms are still in your body, that you are lying or in denial. God is not asking us to deny that sickness exists. God tells us to deny its right to exist in us or have dominion in our lives. Christ has redeemed us from the curse. All sickness is under the curse, and the scriptures plainly tell us that through Christ's work we <u>are</u> and <u>were</u> healed.

Galatians 3:13, 14

> *¹³ Christ hath redeemed us from the curse of the law, being made a curse for us: for it is written, Cursed is every one that hangeth on a tree:*
>
> *¹⁴ That the blessing of Abraham might come on the Gentiles through Jesus Christ; that we might receive the promise of the Spirit through faith.*

When we were born into this world, we were born under the curse. When we were born again, we were redeemed from the curse.

So, when we believe God's report and we, by faith in His Word, take hold of what He has provided for us, we must resist and deny sickness any right to exist in us. We must never forget Isaiah 53:5 which says, *"But he was wounded for our transgressions, he was bruised for our iniquities: the chastisement of our peace was upon him; and with his stripes we are healed."* and 1 Peter 2:24 which says, *"Who his own self bare our sins in his own body on the tree, that we, being dead to sins, should live unto righteousness: by whose stripes ye were healed."*

If sickness did not exist, Jesus would not have had to take our sicknesses at Calvary. But Jesus did something about sickness. Jesus redeemed us and broke the power of sin and sickness. He also broke the power of Satan, their author, and his dominion over us. Now, since He did redeem us, since He finished His work, I refuse, deny and resist that which He has redeemed me from to exist in me or to have dominion in my life. I embrace fully that which He has provided and given to me. I begin to say immediately, "Jesus, you paid the price for me. You bore my sins. You bore my diseases. You defeated my enemy over 2,000 years ago, and I am taking what you have provided for me as mine now. I exalt the Word of my God and the work of my Redeemer above it all." The work that Jesus did is greater than the curse. Find out what Jesus did and do not settle for anything less than what He provided for you.

Every Word that God spoke is true. Let His Word have dominion in your life. Come to that place that you let it govern your life. For if His Word doesn't govern your life, something else will. Jesus asks the Father in John 17:17 to *"Sanctify them through thy truth: thy word is truth."*

Healing is many times a process that begins when you take your healing by faith in the work of Jesus Christ. Then that process continues as you hold fast to His Word, believing and confessing what Christ has done for you. When we do this, we are giving the Holy Spirit of God something to perform in us. Romans 10:10 tells us that *"with the heart man believeth unto righteousness; and with the mouth confession is made unto salvation."*

We can partake of what Jesus Christ has done for us, or we can keep on putting up with what the devil dishes out and fail to receive the many blessings that Christ has made available to us. If you don't partake, you let the blessings pass you by. Christ's work on Calvary revealed that it is God's will for us to walk in total victory on this earth. Let's do it!

Chapter 17

Abraham's Faith

(Our Steps to Follow)

The Bible says, *"The just shall live by his faith."* This truth is found once in the Old Testament (Habakkuk 2:4) and three times in the New Testament (Romans 1:16, 17; Galatians 3:11; Hebrews 10:38).

These scriptures tell us to live by faith, but our level of faith is up to us and not God, and remaining at that level is not automatic. Maintaining and growing our faith is something we must give attention to so it is important to know how faith comes. Romans 10:17 says, *"So then faith cometh by hearing, and hearing by the Word of God."* If you will continue to feed on the Word of God, your faith will grow and prevail (Acts 19:20).

Faith must be lived. Faith is released by speaking and acting on God's Word (Romans 10:10, James 1:22). Bible faith is always referring to believing the gospel. In the New Testament, the Apostle Paul tells us that our faith is to be in the work of Jesus Christ. Jesus Christ is the promised seed through whom all the nations would be blessed. Galatians 3:16 says that Jesus Christ is the seed: *"<u>Now to Abraham and his seed were the promises made</u>. He saith not, And to seeds, as of many; but as of one, And to thy seed, which is Christ."*

God spoke to a man named Abram in the Old Testament. He told him that through his seed all the families of the earth would be blessed.

Abraham's Faith

Genesis 12:1-3

> *¹ Now the Lord had said unto Abram, Get thee out of thy country, and from thy kindred, and from thy father's house, unto a land that I will shew thee:*
>
> *² And I will make of thee a great nation, and I will bless thee, and make thy name great; and thou shalt be a blessing:*
>
> *³ And I will bless them that bless thee, and curse him that curseth thee: and in thee shall all families of the earth be blessed.*

This scripture was pointing to the coming of Jesus Christ - that through Jesus and the work He would do at Calvary, all the nations would be blessed.

God then said to Abram that you shall no longer be called Abram but Abraham which means a "father of a great multitude."

Genesis 17:1-5

> *¹ And when Abram was ninety years old and nine, the Lord appeared to Abram, and said unto him, I am the Almighty God; walk before me, and be thou perfect.*
>
> *² And I will make my covenant between me and thee, and will multiply thee exceedingly.*
>
> *³ And Abram fell on his face: and God talked with him, saying,*
>
> *⁴ As for me, behold, my covenant is with thee, and thou shalt be a father of many nations.*
>
> *⁵ Neither shall thy name any more be called Abram, but thy name shall be Abraham; for a father of many nations have I made thee.*

Believers are told through Paul that we have been justified by faith to receive the blessings of Abraham. We are to know this so we can walk in the faith of Abraham.

Galatians 3:7-9

> *⁷ Know ye therefore that they which are of faith, the same are the children of Abraham.*
>
> *⁸ And the scripture, foreseeing that God would justify the heathen through faith, preached before the gospel unto Abraham, saying, In thee shall all*

nations be blessed.

⁹ So then they which be of faith are blessed with faithful Abraham.

Romans 4 tells us the "Steps of Faith" Abraham took to obtain God's promise.

Abraham believed God.

Romans 4:3 *"For what saith the scripture? <u>Abraham believed God</u>, and it was counted unto him for righteousness."*

When God told Abraham, he would be the father of many nations, Abraham believed what God said. Just as the promise of God was sure to Abraham, His promises are sure to us today by faith placed in the work of Jesus Christ.

Abraham, just like God, called those things which be not as though they were.

Romans 4:17 *"(As it is written, I have made thee a father of many nations,) before him <u>whom he believed</u>, even God, who quickeneth the dead, and <u>calleth those things which be not as though they were</u>."*

One who is in faith calls themselves what God calls them in His Word. We find that after God instructed Abram to start calling himself Abraham that Abraham was no longer trying to talk God into doing what God had promised. Instead, Abraham was working on the receiving end as he continued calling himself what God had called him.

So many people fall short from receiving the promises of God because they believe they cannot proclaim as true something they cannot see or feel. We are not lying when we call ourselves what God calls us. Abram began to call himself Abraham, the "father of a great multitude," as God had instructed him to do. Abraham was calling those things which be not as though they were. If he had not believed God and began to call himself what God had called him, he would <u>never have become</u> what God had said of him. As long as we are <u>not</u> saying what God's Word says about us, there is no agreement and nothing for God to confirm or perform in us. We must get our believing and speaking in line with the Word of God. What has God called you or said about you in His Word that you want to become? Begin to call yourself those things and see them come to pass in your life. If we are not calling ourselves what God calls us in His Word, we are not walking in the steps of Abraham.

Abraham who against hope believed in hope.

Romans 4:18 *"Who against hope believed in hope, that he might become the father of many nations, according to that which was spoken, So, shall thy seed be."*

As I awoke one day, the words, *"Who against hope believed in hope that he might become"* were going over and over in my thoughts. This step really stood out to me since this is a step I had to diligently follow in receiving my healing. Many people never receive God's promises because they cannot be persuaded to believe and call themselves what God says of them in His Word. If I had not done this, I never would have received and seen my healing manifest. Abraham had no rational reason for hope. His body, his age, and Sarah's barrenness were contrary to what Abraham was believing; but Abraham believed God and held fast to his confession of faith for Abraham knew his help wasn't coming from the natural realm, but from the supernatural realm, from the power of Almighty God Himself. Faith will always take you in to receive God's provision when men would say it is impossible, there is no way, there is no hope.

Abraham was not weak in faith.

Romans 4:19 *"And being not weak in faith, he considered not his own body now dead, when he was about an hundred years old, neither yet the deadness of Sarah's womb."*

Weak faith considers the circumstances and the natural realm only. Abraham considered only what God had promised; therefore, he did not grow weak in faith.

Abraham grew strong in faith giving glory to God.

Romans 4:20 *"He staggered not at the promise of God through unbelief; but was strong in faith, giving glory to God."*

On the way to the manifestation of your miracle, offer up a sacrifice of praise which is the fruit of your lips (words of your mouth) giving glory to God (Hebrews 13:15).

Abraham was fully persuaded.

Romans 4:21 *"And being fully persuaded that, what he had promised, he [God] was able also to perform."*

Between the believing and the fulfillment of the promise, you must remain fully persuaded. Abraham had nothing visible to encourage himself, but instead of looking at the circumstances and casting away his confidence, Abraham kept his faith in the Word God had spoken to him. Because he continued to call himself Abraham, as God had told him to do and to consider God's promise rather than the circumstances, he became fully persuaded that God would bring it to pass. Abraham walked out his faith and received God's promise, and his faith in action was counted to him as righteousness.

Romans 4:23-25

> ²³ Now it was <u>not written for his sake alone</u>, that it was imputed to him;
>
> ²⁴ <u>But for us also</u>, to whom it shall be imputed, <u>if we believe on him</u> that raised up Jesus our Lord from the dead;
>
> ²⁵ Who was delivered for our offences, and was raised again for our justification.

And therefore it was <u>imputed to him for righteousness</u>.

These steps are very important and were written for us, the body of Christ, to know and to walk in. As I studied these scriptures about Abraham's faith, these are some of the steps I saw. You may see even more.

1. Know what God has promised.

2. Believe God (His Word).

3. Call those things that be not yet manifest as though they were. (Those walking by sight, reason or head faith [mental assent that God's Word is true] will not do this.)

4. Do not be weak in faith. Do not consider contradictory circumstances. Consider only God's Word.

5. Do not waiver at the promises of God through unbelief.

6. Let your faith grow strong by giving glory and praise to God.

7. Be fully persuaded that God will perform His Word. God is faithful to His Word.

8. Witness the manifestation. (Believing and receiving what God has promised as yours always comes before the manifestation).

This is what Abraham did so that he might become what God had spoken to him. When we follow these same steps, God will bring His promises to pass in our lives too.

Galatians tells us some truths we need to know. We are to know that we have been justified by faith to receive the blessings of Abraham (Galatians 3:7-9)

We are to know that Jesus redeemed us from the curse of the law and made us an heir of all of the blessings.

Galatians 3:13, 14

> *13 Christ hath redeemed us from the curse of the law, being made a curse for us: for it is written, Cursed is every one that hangeth on a tree:*
>
> *14 That the blessing of Abraham might come on the Gentiles through Jesus Christ; that we might receive the promise of the Spirit through faith.*

We are to know that Jesus is the promised seed through whom all the nations would be blessed.

Galatians 3:16 *"Now to Abraham and his seed were the promises made. He saith not, And to seeds, as of many; but as of one, And to thy seed, which is Christ."*

We are to know we are God's children by putting faith in Christ Jesus.

Galatians 3:26 *"For ye are all the children of God by faith in Christ Jesus."*

We are to know we are one in Christ Jesus and heirs according to the promise.

Galatians 3:28, 29

> *28 There is neither Jew nor Greek, there is neither bond nor free, there is neither male nor female: for ye are all one in Christ Jesus.*
>
> *29 And if ye be Christ's, then are ye Abraham's seed, and heirs according to the promise.*

We are to know that God has put receiving His provisions solely on the basis of faith to make it sure to all the seed whether they be of the circumcision or of the uncircumcision, old covenant or new covenant, and so on. And that through faith the promises are sure to all who will believe

and live out their faith.

Romans 4:12, 16

> *[12] And the father of circumcision to them who are not of the circumcision only, but <u>who also walk in the steps of that faith of our father Abraham</u>, which he had being yet uncircumcised.*
>
> *[16] Therefore <u>it is of faith</u>, that it might be by grace; to the end <u>the promise might be sure to all the seed</u>; not to that only which is of the law, but to that also which is of the faith of Abraham; who is the father of us all.*

Faith believes God and says about themselves what God says about them in His Word. Start calling yourself what God calls you if you want to experience God's promises in your life. We can call ourselves the redeemed because Psalm 107:2 says, *"Let the redeemed of the Lord say so, whom he hath redeemed from the hand of the enemy."* All sickness is under the curse as shown in Deuteronomy 28, and since Jesus redeemed us from the curse (Galatians 3:13, 14), you can say, "I'm redeemed from the curse of that disease." Call yourself the healed by Jesus stripes (Isaiah 53:5, 1 Peter 2:24). One who is in faith calls those things that are not yet seen as though they were.

In creation, God called those things that be not as though they were.

Genesis 1:1-3

> *[1] In the beginning God created the heaven and the earth*
>
> *[2] And the earth was without form, and void; and darkness was upon the face of the deep. And the Spirit of God moved upon the face of the waters.*
>
> *[3] And God said, <u>Let there be light: and there was light</u>.*

The world we live in was <u>spoken</u> into existence by God.

Hebrews 11:3 *"Through faith we understand that <u>the worlds were framed by the word of God</u>, so that things which are seen were not made of things which do appear."*

All the prophets called those things that were not seen when they foretold of the coming of Jesus Christ throughout the Old Testament. (Isaiah 46:10).

Jesus tells us to do this.

Mark 11:23, 24

> *23 For verily I say unto you, That whosoever shall say unto this mountain, Be thou removed, and be thou cast into the sea; and shall not doubt in his heart, but shall believe that those things which he saith shall come to pass; he shall have whatsoever he saith.*

> *24 Therefore I say unto you, What things soever ye desire, when ye pray, believe that ye receive them, and ye shall have them.*

Paul said the Spirit of faith does this.

2 Corinthians 4:13 *"We having the same spirit of faith, according as it is written, I believed, and therefore have I spoken; we also believe, and therefore speak."*

Paul also tells us where faith looks and where our faith focus should be.

2 Corinthians 4:18 *"While we look not at the things which are seen, but at the things which are not seen: for the things which are seen are temporal; but the things which are not seen are eternal."*

Hebrews 12:2 *"Looking unto Jesus the author and finisher of our faith; who for the joy that was set before him endured the cross, despising the shame, and is set down at the right hand of the throne of God."*

The Bible tells us the importance of confessing our faith.

Hebrews 10:23 *"Let us hold fast the profession [confession] of our faith without wavering; (for he is faithful that promised)."*

In Revelation 12:11 the Apostle John sees from heaven's viewpoint how we overcome Satan and all of his works. It is by the blood of the lamb (Jesus Christ) and the words of our mouth confessing what God's Word says about us.

Jesus is called the Apostle and High Priest of our profession (confession) of faith.

Hebrews 4:14-16

> *14 Seeing then that we have a great high priest, that is passed into the heavens, Jesus the Son of God, let us hold fast our profession.*

¹⁵ For we have not an high priest which cannot be touched with the feeling of our infirmities; but was in all points tempted like as we are, yet without sin.

¹⁶ <u>Let us therefore come boldly unto the throne of grace</u>, that we may obtain mercy, and find grace to help in time of need.

Because Jesus is the Word made flesh and has been made wisdom to us (John 1:1-4, 14; 1 Corinthians 1:30); and His Word is the eternal wisdom of God spoken to us (Proverbs 2:6, 7), it must be the basis of our faith. There is nothing more real or sure than God's Word.

The Bible says it is God's Word that gives us faith.

Romans 10:17 *"So then faith cometh by hearing and hearing by the word of God."*

Then for faith to produce the end result, God's Word must be believed and received in our hearts. Our very entrance into the kingdom of God is by grace through faith (Ephesians 2:8, 9). We also enter into all the promises and provisions Christ obtained for us in this same way.

The Bible gives us the definition of faith.

Hebrews 11:1 *"Now faith is the substance of things hoped for, the evidence of things not seen.*

The original text says, *"not yet revealed to the physical senses."*

Bible faith is not mere mental belief or acceptance that God's Word is true. It is believing in your heart (spirit) what God has said in His Word, trusting in it, accepting it, adhering to it, committing to it and doing it. This is true Bible faith. This is receiving faith. If anyone's believing is based on their natural senses, human reasoning or even mental assent that the Word of God is true, this is not Bible faith; therefore, it is not receiving faith. To walk by faith, we must walk by God's Word. We must exalt God's Word above sight, feeling or any reasoning that opposes God's Word. Our faith is not based on what we see with our natural eyes, but upon what we see in the Word of God (2 Corinthians 5:7). Every born-again believer is an heir of the total work of Jesus Christ, and God is still confirming His Word today for those who will believe, act upon and hold fast to His Word. Yes, it matters whether or not we live by faith and it matters whether or not we live out our faith.

James 2:17, 19, 26

> *17 Even so <u>faith, if it hath not works, is dead,</u> being alone.*
>
> *19 Thou believest that there is one God; thou doest well: the devils also believe, and tremble.*
>
> *26 For as the body without the spirit is dead, so faith without works [corresponding action] is dead also.*

We will never be called upon to believe for something more difficult than Abraham was called upon to believe. Even though the promise God spoke was in the future, Abraham's faith in action had to be now. He believed, called himself Abraham, and did not waver until he saw God's promise with his eyes. Today we are to walk by faith in the finished work of Jesus Christ at Calvary. We are to believe and put our faith in action until we see God's promise in our lives.

The principles of faith are the same for all of God's promises. Faith must be released through words from your mouth. Faith calls those things that be not as though they were. Romans 10:10 says, *"For with the heart man believeth unto righteousness; and with the mouth confession is made <u>unto</u> salvation."*

Unto: Thereunto, to or into indicating the point reached or entered of place or purpose, result – expressing motion. (*Strong's Exhaustive Concordance*).

Our faith should always be growing. As born-again believers, we are authorized to call the promises of God ours because we have become heirs of all the finished work of Jesus Christ. When we know we have taken God at His Word and the promise belongs to us, we can then confess it as ours until it manifests in our lives.

God is not saying "no" to His promises when He has already said "yes." 2 Corinthians 1:20 says, *"For all the promises of God in him are yea, and in him [Christ Jesus] Amen, unto the glory of God by us."*

We must agree with what God's Word says about us to receive His promises. To stay in agreement with God, we must get rid of all unbelief, which is believing contrary to what God has spoken. We must get unbelief out of our hearts and out of our mouths. We must uproot it! We must reject it! Contrary thoughts, unbelief, and doubts must be cast down. If you follow Abraham's steps of faith, you too will see God's promises manifested in your life.

Chapter 18

Holy Spirit Promised

While the first part of this book dealt mainly with walking in the healing provision and total salvation that Jesus Christ provided for us, the next few chapters will be about the Holy Spirit and His power in the believer's life.

The Holy Spirit has always worked with the Father and with the Son of God, both in the creation of the universe and of mankind (Genesis 1:26-28) as well as the virgin birth (Luke 1:35), when Jesus the Word was made flesh (John 1:14). Even in ministry the Holy Spirit worked with Jesus. The Holy Spirit has been part of every new birth of believers, every miracle and healing, and every victory you experience in this life. And it is He who will catch away the church (1 Thessalonians 4:13-17).

God the Father, Jesus, the Son, and the Holy Spirit are called the Godhead in Acts 17:29, Romans 1:20 and Colossians 2:9. 1 John 5:7 says, *"For there are three that bear record in heaven, the Father, the Word, and the Holy Ghost: and these three are one."* The three have always worked together in purpose, plan, and will; and they never work contrary to one other.

The prophets of the Old Covenant spoke of the time when Jesus, the Christ, the Messiah, would come and establish the New Covenant and declared that the Holy Spirit would indwell every born-again believer. This promise, which was to be a future event, began at Pentecost (Acts 2) with the outpouring of the Holy Ghost. It continued throughout the New Testament and will continue as long as men can call on the Lord and be saved. This promise is until the end of the church age.

It was also foretold by the Prophet Ezekiel.

Ezekiel 36:25-27

> *25 Then will I sprinkle clean water upon you, and ye shall be clean: from all your filthiness, and from all your idols, will I cleanse you.*
>
> *26 A new heart also will I give you, and a new spirit will I put within you: and I will take away the stony heart out of your flesh, and I will give you an heart of flesh.*
>
> *27 And I will put my spirit within you, and cause you to walk in my statutes, and ye shall keep my judgments, and do them.*

God's Prophet Joel prophesied that in the latter days God's Spirit would be poured out on all flesh.

Joel 2:28, 29, 32

> *28 And it shall come to pass afterward, that I will pour out my spirit upon all flesh; and your sons and your daughters shall prophesy, your old men shall dream dreams, your young men shall see visions:*
>
> *29 And also upon the servants and upon the handmaids in those days will I pour out my spirit.*
>
> *32 And it shall come to pass, that whosoever shall call on the name of the Lord shall be delivered: for in mount Zion and in Jerusalem shall be deliverance, as the Lord hath said, and in the remnant whom the Lord shall call.*

Now, let's see what the New Testament has to say about the coming of the Holy Ghost.

John the Baptist

Matthew 3:1, 5, 6, 11

> *1 In those days came John the Baptist, preaching in the wilderness of Judaea,*
>
> *5 Then went out to him Jerusalem, and all Judaea, and all the region round about Jordan,*

⁶ And were baptized of him in Jordan, confessing their sins.

¹¹ I indeed baptize you with water unto repentance. but he that cometh after me is mightier than I, whose shoes I am not worthy to bear: he shall baptize you with the Holy Ghost, and with fire.

As I was studying verse 11, the Holy Spirit spoke this to my spirit saying, "John made this promise to the <u>multitude</u> gathered there from the various cities. This was not just for the apostles to get the church started, which some have been taught to believe, because the apostles had not yet been chosen since Jesus' ministry had not yet begun. No, this promise was for all the people who were gathered there that day as well as for all believers to come.

Before Jesus began His earthly ministry, He was baptized and the Holy Spirit descended upon Him (Luke 3:22). He was then led of the Spirit into the wilderness to be tempted of the devil (Luke 4:1) and afterwards returned in the power of the Spirit to do the work of the ministry (Luke 4:14, 18-21; Acts 10:38). Jesus, in His earthly ministry, had to be anointed by the Holy Spirit because He had laid down His divinity and became as a man (Philippians 2:6-9). The same Holy Spirit now works with believers today empowering them to do the works God has called them to do. The Holy Spirit confirms the Word with signs following (John 14:12, Mark 16:15-20).

God said that the promise of the Holy Spirit is to all believers. Jesus promised the Holy Spirit to large crowds gathered for Passover.

John 7:37, 38

³⁷ In the last day, that great day of the feast, Jesus stood and cried, saying, <u>If any man thirst, let him come unto me, and drink.</u>

³⁸ <u>He that believeth on me,</u> as the scripture hath said, <u>out of his belly shall flow rivers of living water.</u>

We must believe the Word of God regardless of what any other person says. John 7:39 says, *"(But this spake he of the Spirit, which they that believe on him <u>should</u> receive: for the Holy Ghost was not yet given; because that Jesus was not yet glorified.)"* In this verse, Jesus said they **should receive**, <u>not they **could receive**</u>.

So, why could they not be filled that day? Jesus told us why. Because Jesus had not yet finished His earthly mission. He had not yet become our sin-bearer nor been delivered up to the cross for our offenses and raised up again to justify us. The "us" is everyone who would believe in His substitutionary work (Romans 4:25; John 3:14-17; Acts 3:13; 13:38, 39; 2 Corinthians 5:21; Romans 3:20-26).

Jesus fulfilled all that was written of Him in the law of Moses, the book of the prophets and the Psalms (Luke 24:44-49). Jesus has now finished His earthly mission in redeeming mankind. He paid our sin debt so everyone who would believe in Him and His work would be cleared of all sin and guilt, made righteous and be in right standing with God, and would pass from the spiritual death which occurred in the fall of mankind through the sin of man in the garden into eternal life. Now, through Christ Jesus' work, whosoever will can be born again from above and pass from spiritual death to eternal life (John 3:5, 6, 36, 5:24; Ephesians 2:1-5, 8, 9).

Oh, the wonder of it all! Jesus has accomplished all this and been glorified. So now all who are thirsty and believe on Jesus can **and should** be filled with the Holy Ghost. This promise still stands today.

In John 14 Jesus again promises to send the Holy Spirit to dwell in us. Jesus said when He had finished His work at Calvary, He would go back to the Father to prepare a place for us and then would come again to receive us to Himself. All Christians believe this part of Chapter 14; and if this promise is true for all believers, which it is, so is every promise that is made in Chapter 14, including verse 12.

John 14:12 says, *"Verily, verily, I say unto you, He that believeth on me, the works that I do shall he do also; and greater works than these shall he do; because I go unto my Father."*

Jesus tells us of the works the ones who believe on Him would do.

Mark 16:17, 18

> *[17] And these signs shall follow them that believe; In my name shall they cast out devils; they shall speak with new tongues;*
>
> *[18] They shall take up serpents; and if they drink any deadly thing, it shall not hurt them; they shall lay hands on the sick, and they shall recover.*

John 14 tells us how we will do these works. It will not be by man's natural ability, but by the Holy Spirit's supernatural ability enabling us (Zechariah

4:6) just as He enabled Jesus to do the works He did in Acts 10:38, *"How God anointed Jesus of Nazareth with the Holy Ghost and with power: who went about doing good, and healing all that were oppressed of the devil; for God was with him."*

This infilling of the Holy Ghost in believers is the same Holy Ghost that anointed Jesus and will enable us to do what the Father has called us to do because the Holy Spirit will be our teacher of the things of God. Studying and meditating on John 14 will help the believer see and better understand what Jesus is telling us.

Jesus said in John 14:16, *"And I will pray the Father, and he shall give you another Comforter, that he may abide with you forever."*

Jesus then tells us who the Comforter is.

John 14:25, 26

> *25 These things have I spoken unto you, being yet present with you.*
>
> *26 But the Comforter, which is the Holy Ghost, whom the Father will send in my name, he shall teach you all things, and bring all things to your remembrance, whatsoever I have said unto you.*

We cannot receive the Holy Spirit until we are born again as we see in John 14:17, *"Even the Spirit of truth; whom the world [sinners] cannot receive, because it seeth him not, neither knoweth him: but ye know him; for he dwelleth with you, and shall be in you."* We can see from this verse the promise of the Holy Spirit's infilling is not for sinners, but for believers only. However, when the world believes on Jesus and receives Him as Lord, they can have eternal life and then receive the infilling of the Holy Spirit as Jesus tells Nicodemus in John 3:3-6, 14-17.

In John 14:20 Jesus tells us, *"At that day ye shall know that I am in my Father, and ye in me, and I in you."* Then we are told in John 15:26, *"But when the Comforter is come, whom I will send unto you from the Father, even the Spirit of truth, which proceedeth from the Father, he shall testify of me."*

Jesus said in John 16:7, *"Nevertheless I tell you the truth; It is expedient for you that I go away: for if I go not away, the Comforter will not come unto you; but if I depart, I will send him unto you."* Then in John 16:13 Jesus tells us the Holy Spirit will guide us *"into all truth: for he shall not speak of himself; but what-*

soever he shall hear, that shall he speak: and he will shew you things to come." Continuing in verse 14, Jesus tells us that *"He shall glorify me [Jesus]: for he shall receive of mine, and shall shew it unto you."*

After the Lord Jesus had finished his earthly mission of the redemption of fallen man and was ready to ascend back to be seated at the right hand of the Father, we see Jesus' last instruction to the ones gathered there.

Acts 1:4, 5, 8, 9

> *[4] And, being assembled together with them, commanded them that they should not depart from Jerusalem, but <u>wait for the promise of the Father</u>, which, saith he, ye have heard of me.*
>
> *[5] For John truly baptized with water; but ye shall be baptized with the Holy Ghost not many days hence.*
>
> *[8] <u>But ye shall receive power, after that the Holy Ghost is come upon you</u>: and ye shall be witnesses unto me both in Jerusalem, and in all Judaea, and in Samaria, and unto the uttermost part of the earth.*
>
> *[9] And when he had spoken these things, while they beheld, he was taken up; and a cloud received him out of their sight.*

Notice Jesus' last commandment was that they should not depart Jerusalem but <u>wait for the promise of the Father,</u> which was being baptized in the power of the Holy Ghost.

In the next chapter, we will see the Holy Ghost being poured out as promised.

Chapter 19

Holy Spirit Given to New Testament Saints (Outpourings)

Remember, God, through His prophets, spoke of the promise of the Holy Ghost.

Joel 2:28-32

> *28 And it shall come to pass afterward, that I will pour out my spirit upon all flesh; and your sons and your daughters shall prophesy, your old men shall dream dreams, your young men shall see visions:*
>
> *29 And also upon the servants and upon the handmaids in those days will I pour out my spirit.*
>
> *30 And I will shew wonders in the heavens and in the earth, blood, and fire, and pillars of smoke.*
>
> *31 The sun shall be turned into darkness, and the moon into blood, before the great and terrible day of the Lord come.*
>
> *32 And it shall come to pass, that whosoever shall call on the name of the Lord shall be delivered: for in mount Zion and in Jerusalem shall be deliverance, as the Lord hath said, and in the remnant whom the Lord shall call.*

The early saints honored the Holy Spirit of God and His work. They welcomed Him. They depended upon Him for guidance, empowerment, and help in all they did.

Jesus tells us in Acts 1:8, *"But ye shall receive power, after that the Holy Ghost is come upon you: and ye shall be witnesses unto me both in Jerusalem, and in all Judaea, and in Samaria, and unto the uttermost part of the earth."*

As I studied Acts 1:8, I recalled this is what John the Baptist had <u>told the vast multitude gathered to hear him</u> (Matthew 3:5). John the Baptist said in Matthew 3:11, *"I indeed baptize you with water unto repentance. But he [Jesus] that cometh after me is mightier than I, whose shoes I am not worthy to bear: he shall baptize you with the Holy Ghost, and with fire."* Notice this promise to which Jesus now makes reference was promised not to just a few but to the <u>vast multitude</u> gathered there.

We see what happened for those who obeyed the command that Jesus had given. All those who went to the upper room to wait to be filled with the Holy Spirit left that day speaking in other tongues that they themselves had not learned, but they were speaking by utterance from the Holy Spirit of God.

Acts 1:13, 14

> *13 And when they were come in, they went up into an upper room, where abode both Peter, and James, and John, and Andrew, Philip, and Thomas, Bartholomew, and Matthew, James the son of Alphaeus, and Simon Zelotes, and Judas the brother of James.*
>
> *14 These all continued with one accord in prayer and supplication, with the women, and **<u>Mary the mother of Jesus</u>,** and with his brethren.*

The number who went to the upper room, both men and women, were 120. This included Mary, the mother of Jesus, who went to the upper room to receive the baptism of the Holy Ghost. Then we see in Acts 2 the coming of the Holy Spirit just as promised. Let's look at what happened on the Day of Pentecost when the Holy Ghost was poured out on the believers in the upper room.

Acts 2:1-4

> *1 And when the day of Pentecost was fully come, they were all with one accord in one place.*

² And suddenly there came a sound from heaven as of a rushing mighty wind, and it filled all the house where they were sitting.

³ And there appeared unto them cloven tongues like as of fire, and it sat upon each of them.

⁴ And they were all filled with the Holy Ghost, and began to speak with other tongues, as the Spirit gave them utterance.

They were speaking words given to them by the Holy Spirit - words unknown by those speaking but understood by the hearers. Then we see those gathered in Jerusalem that day were devout men *"out of every nation under heaven."*

Acts: 2:5-13

⁵ And there were dwelling at Jerusalem Jews, devout men, out of every nation under heaven.

⁶ Now when this was noised abroad, the multitude came together, and were confounded, because that every man heard them speak in his own language.

⁷ And they were all amazed and marvelled, saying one to another, Behold, are not all these which speak Galilaeans?

⁸ And how hear we every man in our own tongue, wherein we were born?

⁹ Parthians, and Medes, and Elamites, and the dwellers in Mesopotamia, and in Judaea, and Cappadocia, in Pontus, and Asia,

¹⁰ Phrygia, and Pamphylia, in Egypt, and in the parts of Libya about Cyrene, and strangers of Rome, Jews and proselytes,

¹¹ Cretes and Arabians, we do hear them speak in our tongues the wonderful works of God.

¹² And they were all amazed, and were in doubt, saying one to another, What meaneth this?

¹³ Others mocking said, These men are full of new wine.

Speaking in tongues came that day when they were filled and still comes now when we are filled with the Holy Spirit. Some still mock speaking in tongues, but it doesn't change the truth that this was and is from God. Some deny speaking in tongues is part of being filled with the Spirit, but notice it is the Spirit of God that gives the utterance. When anyone receives this infilling in the Holy Spirit, speaking in tongues will be a part of it. It is not all there is to it, but it is an important part of being filled with the Holy Spirit.

Peter stood up that day and said that these men are not drunk as you suppose (Acts 2:15). Then he went on to say:

Acts 2:16-21

16 But this is that which was spoken by the prophet Joel;

17 And it shall come to pass in the last days, saith God, I will pour out of my Spirit upon all flesh: and your sons and your daughters shall prophesy, and your young men shall see visions, and your old men shall dream dreams:

18 And on my servants and on my handmaidens I will pour out in those days of my Spirit; and they shall prophesy:

19 And I will shew wonders in heaven above, and signs in the earth beneath; blood, and fire, and vapor of smoke:

20 The sun shall be turned into darkness, and the moon into blood, before the great and notable day of the Lord come:

21 And it shall come to pass, that whosoever shall call on the name of the Lord shall be saved.

We can see by these scriptures that what Peter stood up and spoke that day verified what Joel had prophesied of the promise made of the Holy Spirit coming and that His works would be here as long as men can call upon the name of the Lord and be saved.

When we receive the Holy Spirit today, which again Jesus said those who believe on Him should (John 7:37-39), we receive the same Holy Spirit that came to fill all who were gathered in the upper room at the beginning of the Church Age (Acts 2:1-4). This is the same Holy Spirit Who is still here in the earth today performing the works of God and will be here for the entire time that salvation is offered to mankind and as long as the church is in the world.

Peter told the large crowd gathered there that this promise is to you and your children and to all that come to Him in the future.

Acts 2:32, 33, 36-39

³² This Jesus hath God raised up, whereof we all are witnesses.

³³ Therefore being by the right hand of God exalted, and having received of the Father the promise of the Holy Ghost, he hath shed forth this, which ye now see and hear.

³⁶ Therefore let all the house of Israel know assuredly, that God hath made the same Jesus, whom ye have crucified, both Lord and Christ.

³⁷ Now when they heard this, they were pricked in their heart, and said unto Peter and to the rest of the apostles, Men and brethren, what shall we do?

³⁸ Then Peter said unto them, Repent, and be baptized every one of you in the name of Jesus Christ for the remission of sins, and ye shall receive the gift of the Holy Ghost.

³⁹ For the promise is unto you, and to your children, and to all that are afar off, even as many as the Lord our God shall call.

God calls everyone to be saved, but not everyone responds. How do I know that? Because it says in 1 Timothy 2:4 that God would have all men to be saved and 2 Peter 3:9 says God is not willing that any perish.

Peter told them that the promise was for those gathered there that day and the promise is also for us today. What was the promise? It was the same in-filling of the Holy Spirit they had just witnessed. Once when I was studying these scriptures, the Holy Spirit spoke to my spirit and said, "God gave the promise, and try as they may man cannot rescind it." God has not authorized any man to change His Word; neither has He given this authority to any denomination, preacher, or teacher to change His Word. No one can set aside or amend any portion of God's Word, nor do we have any power to cancel any portion of this gospel. Yet, some have dared to do so. They have even denied the works the Holy Spirit came to do. They say, "This is not for us today." Hebrews 13:8 still declares, *"Jesus Christ the same yesterday, and to day, and for ever."* So, what He did yesterday, He is still doing today and will continue to do tomorrow. The Holy Spirit did not come to stay for just a while. He came to stay and empower believers for the entire time that salvation is offered to mankind and as long as the church is in the world.

Now let's continue looking in the Book of Acts, Chapter 8, where others were filled with the Holy Ghost.

Acts 8:5, 12, 14-17

> [5] *Then Philip went down to the city of Samaria, and preached Christ unto them.*
>
> [12] *When they believed Philip preaching the things concerning the kingdom of God, and the name of Jesus Christ, they were baptized, both men and women.*
>
> [14] *Now when the apostles which were at Jerusalem heard that Samaria had received the word of God, they sent unto them Peter and John:*
>
> [15] *Who, when they were come down, prayed for them, that they might receive the Holy Ghost:*
>
> [16] *(For as yet he was fallen upon none of them: only they were baptized in the name of the Lord Jesus.)*
>
> [17] *Then laid they their hands on them, and they received the Holy Ghost.*

We see that after the people of Samaria had received Christ, they still needed to be filled with the Holy Spirit. They received the Holy Spirit only after Peter and John laid hands on them.

Saul, later called Paul, received the Holy Spirit after the disciple Ananias laid hands on him.

Acts 9:17, 18

> [17] *And Ananias went his way, and entered into the house; and putting his hands on him said, Brother Saul, the Lord, even Jesus, that appeared unto thee in the way as thou camest, hath sent me, that thou mightest receive thy sight, and be filled with the Holy Ghost.*
>
> [18] *And immediately there fell from his eyes as it had been scales: and he received sight forthwith, and arose, and was baptized.*

In Acts 10 Peter preached to the Gentiles at Cornelius' house, and they received the baptism of the Holy Spirit as believers are still receiving today.

Acts 10:24, 27, 44-48

> [24] *And the morrow after they entered into Caesarea. And Cornelius waited for them, and he had called together his kinsmen and near friends.*

²⁷ And as he [Peter] talked with him [Cornelius], he went in, and <u>found many that were come together</u>.

⁴⁴ While Peter yet spake these words, <u>the Holy Ghost fell on all them which heard the word</u>.

⁴⁵ And they of the circumcision which believed were astonished, as many as came with Peter, because that on the Gentiles also was poured out the gift of the Holy Ghost.

⁴⁶ <u>For they heard them speak with tongues, and magnify God</u>. Then answered Peter,

⁴⁷ Can any man forbid water, that these should not be baptized, which have received the Holy Ghost as well as we?

⁴⁸ And he commanded them to be baptized in the name of the Lord.

Paul on his visit to Ephesus asked some disciples he met if they had received the Holy Ghost? He asked because he knew they needed to be baptized in the Holy Ghost. Then Apostle Paul laid hands on them, and they received the promised Holy Ghost.

Acts 19:1-6

¹ And it came to pass, that, while Apollos was at Corinth, Paul having passed through the upper coasts came to Ephesus: and finding certain disciples,

² He said unto them, <u>Have ye received the Holy Ghost since ye believed? And they said unto him, We have not so much as heard whether there be any Holy Ghost</u>.

³ And he said unto them, Unto what then were ye baptized? And they said, Unto John's baptism.

⁴ Then said Paul, John verily baptized with the baptism of repentance, saying unto the people, that they should believe on him which should come after him, that is, on Christ Jesus.

⁵ When they heard this, they were baptized in the name of the Lord Jesus.

⁶ And <u>when Paul had laid his hands upon them, the Holy Ghost came on them; and they spake with tongues, and prophesied</u>.

In the next chapter, we will see some of the workings of the Holy Ghost in the church.

Chapter 20

Holy Spirit at Work in the Church

Let's look at the works that have been and continue to be performed by the Holy Spirit.

Jesus told Nicodemus that our new birth into the kingdom of God is by the Holy Spirit.

John 3:5 *"Jesus answered, Verily, verily, I say unto thee, Except a man be born of water and of the Spirit, he cannot enter into the kingdom of God."*

Jesus said the Holy Spirit will be our Comforter.

The Amplified Classic edition tells us more.

John 14:16 *"And I will ask the Father, and He will give you another Comforter (Counselor, Helper, Intercessor, Advocate, Strengthener, and Standby), that He may remain with you forever."*

The Holy Spirit is:

- Counselor
- Helper
- Intercessor
- Advocate
- Strengthener
- Standby

…and will be with us forever!

In addition to the new birth, the Holy Spirit also performs healing and all the parts of salvation (Rescue or safety [physical or morally]: Deliver, health, save, saving). This is all part of His work as well as teacher, guide, enabler, revealer, helper and so forth. He is one with the Father; He is one with the Son, Jesus Christ (1 John 5:7); and they have always worked together as one.

Jesus said the Comforter (Holy Spirit) would guide us into all truth.

John 16:13 *"Howbeit when he, the Spirit of truth, is come, he will guide you into all truth: for he shall not speak of himself; but whatsoever he shall hear, that shall he speak: and he will shew you things to come."*

Jesus said the Holy Spirit will glorify Him (Jesus)

John 16:14 *"He shall glorify me: for he shall receive of mine, and shall shew it unto you."*

The church is the body of Christ (Ephesians 1:22, 23) and was born in the power of the Spirit, ministered in the power of the Spirit and will be caught away in the rapture of the church by the power of the Holy Spirit.

Being full of the Holy Spirit was essential in choosing men to serve in the church.

Acts 6:2-4

> ² *Then the twelve called the multitude of the disciples unto them, and said, It is not reason that we should leave the word of God, and serve tables.*
>
> ³ *Wherefore, brethren, look ye out among you seven men of honest report, full of the Holy Ghost and wisdom, whom we may appoint over this business.*
>
> ⁴ *But we will give ourselves continually to prayer, and to the ministry of the word.*

Now let's look at Acts 2:17, where the Apostle Peter said that this promise is for the "last days." *"And it shall come to pass in the last days, saith God, I will pour out of my Spirit upon all flesh: and your sons and your daughters shall* *prophesy, and your young men shall see visions, and your old men shall dream dreams."* The scripture reveals to us that the last days is a time element.

The Bible tells us when the last days began.

Hebrews 1:1, 2

> *¹ God, who at sundry times and in divers manners spake in time past unto the fathers by the prophets,*
>
> *² Hath in these last days spoken unto us by his Son, whom he hath appointed heir of all things, by whom also he made the worlds.*

The word "last" is defined as farthest, final (of place or time): of, last, latter end, uttermost *(Strong's Exhaustive Concordance).*

The last days are also referred to as *"these last times"* in 1 Peter 1:20 which says, *"Who verily was foreordained before the foundation of the world, but was manifest in these last times for you."*

In 1 Corinthians, Chapters 12-14, Paul tells the body of Christ (the church), about the spiritual gifts of the Holy Spirit that God has set in the church and says He does not want us to be ignorant about these truths (1 Corinthians 12:1). The spiritual gifts are listed in the following verses.

1 Corinthians 12:4-13

> *⁴ Now there are diversities of gifts, but the same Spirit [Holy Spirit].*
>
> *⁵ And there are differences of administrations, but the same Lord.*
>
> *⁶ And there are diversities of operations, but it is the same God which worketh all in all.*
>
> *⁷ But the manifestation of the Spirit is given to every man to profit withal.*
>
> *⁸ For to one is given by the Spirit the word of wisdom; to another the word of knowledge by the same Spirit;*
>
> *⁹ To another faith by the same Spirit; to another the gifts of healing by the same Spirit;*
>
> *¹⁰ To another the working of miracles; to another prophecy; to another discerning of spirits; to another divers kinds of tongues; to another the interpretation of tongues:*
>
> *¹¹ But all these worketh that one and the selfsame Spirit, dividing to every*

man severally as he will.

¹² For as the body is one, and hath many members, and all the members of that one body, being many, are one body: so also is Christ.

¹³ <u>For by one Spirit are we all baptized into one body</u>, whether we be Jews or Gentiles, whether we be bond or free; and have been all made to drink into one Spirit.

Notice in verses 8-10 that the Apostle Paul lists <u>nine gifts of the Holy Spirit</u>. Some have categorized them as three power gifts, three vocal gifts, and three revelation gifts. All of these gifts still operate in the church today - or at least they should. Also, notice the Apostle Paul tells us that they are given by the Spirit of God.

In verse 12 the Apostle Paul uses the analogy of the physical body to explain the working together of the gifts of the Holy Spirit in the church. Just as all parts of the physical body are vital and necessary to the function of the body, so are the gifts God has set in the church vital and necessary to Christ's spiritual body, which is the church.

While no one would deny that all the human body parts are vital to the function of the human body, some have denied that these <u>nine spiritual gifts</u> are still necessary in Christ's spiritual body (the church). But Paul makes it clear how vital all spiritual gifts are to the church and how they function.

1 Corinthians 12:28-30

²⁸ And God hath set some in the church, first apostles, secondarily prophets, thirdly teachers, after that miracles, then gifts of healings, helps, governments, diversities of tongues.

²⁹ Are all apostles? are all prophets? are all teachers? are all workers of miracles?

³⁰ Have all the gifts of healing? do all speak with tongues? do all interpret?

Notice that in this chapter as in Chapters 11 and 15 of 1 Corinthians, Paul is not trying to do away with the gifts and their function in the church, but rather is setting them in order as to how they should work and the benefit thereof. God is the one who set the gifts in the church to benefit the church, and man cannot remove them.

The Amplified Classic Edition of 1 Corinthians 14 makes it clear that prophecy and tongues are an integral part of the church today.

1 Corinthians 14:39, 40

> *39 So [to conclude], my brethren, earnestly desire and set your hearts on prophesying (on being inspired to preach and teach and to interpret God's will and purpose), and do not forbid or hinder speaking in [unknown] tongues.*
>
> *40 But all things should be done with regard to decency and propriety and in an orderly fashion.*

Many deny these spiritual gifts and do not desire them as we are instructed to do in 1 Corinthians 12:31, *"But covet earnestly the best gifts: and yet shew I unto you a more excellent way."* That is why these gifts do not operate in many of the churches or in many of the believers' lives today. God did not remove the gifts; but if you do not believe in them or desire them, they will not operate in your life.

Tongues referred to in 1 Corinthians 12:30 is one of the gifts mentioned earlier in 1 Corinthians 12:10 which should have an interpretation. The Apostle Paul is not speaking of the believer's individual prayer language here, which we who are filled with the Holy Spirit should yield to in prayer (Jude 20; Romans 8:26, 27; Ephesians 6:18; 1 Corinthians 14:2, 4, 14, 15).

In 1 Corinthians 13, Paul tells us how the gifts of the Spirit should work. Here, as in other places, he is stressing the importance of love. This chapter is sometimes used by those trying to convince others that the gifts of the Holy Spirit are no longer needed nor operate today. Again, the Apostle Paul is not trying to do away with the gifts, but rather he is telling us that operating in love is needed to have these gifts work effectively in the church and in one's life.

Notice in 1 Corinthians 13:2 the Apostle Paul did not say the gift of prophecy or the word of knowledge should not operate today, *"And though I have the gift of prophecy, and understand all mysteries, and all knowledge; and though I have all faith, so that I could remove mountains, and have not charity [love], I am nothing."* The Apostle Paul is saying that without love, these gifts are of no personal benefit.

In 1 Corinthians 13:8 after the Apostle Paul says the love of God will never fail, he tells us when the gifts of prophecy, knowledge and tongues will cease, *"Charity [Love] never faileth: but whether there be prophecies, they shall fail* (He says, 'shall fail,' not that they have failed)*; whether there be tongues, they shall cease* (again, it says 'shall cease,' not have ceased)*; whether there be knowledge, it shall vanish away."*

Some teach that tongues have ceased based on reading this passage as if it says, "have ceased," but they don't say anything about knowledge having ceased. If tongues have ceased, then knowledge must have ceased also based on the reading of this passage. We know that is not true. Paul is speaking here of the "now" period of time. This "now" extends from the time this scripture was written and for as long as the church is in the world. Since this has not happened as yet, these gifts have not ceased as yet and should still be functioning in the church today.

Let's continue in 1 Corinthians 13:9, 10, 12, where Paul is speaking of "now."

> [9] *For we know in part, and we prophesy in part,*
>
> [10] *But when that which is perfect is come, then that which is in part shall be done away.*
>
> [12] *For now we see through a glass, darkly; but then face to face: now I know in part; but then shall I know even as also I am known.*

In these scriptures, the *"then"* Paul is talking about is when we see Jesus face to face.

Psalm 17:15 *"As for me, I will behold thy face in righteousness: I shall be satisfied, when I awake, with thy likeness."*

1 John 3:2 *"Beloved, now are we the sons of God, and it doth not yet appear what we shall be: but we know that, when he shall appear, we shall be like him; for we shall see him as he is."*

Revelation 22:4 *"And they shall see his face; and his name shall be in their foreheads."*

Note: We are currently in the <u>now</u> period of time and not the <u>then</u> period of time.

In 1 Corinthians 13:13 the gifts of the Spirit have not vanished nor ceased.

This scripture says that faith, hope, and love abide. These three are needed for the Word of God and the gifts of the Spirit to function as they ought to in the believer's life. When we are in heaven, these gifts God placed in the church to help us in our earthly walk will no longer be needed.

I personally believe that in heaven we will all speak in one tongue, not different tongues or languages. I believe we will all speak and understand the language of the Holy Spirit.

After the Apostle Paul set in order how the gifts should function in the church, he says in 1 Corinthians 14:1 to *"follow after charity, and desire spiritual gifts, but rather that ye may prophesy."* To prophesy is one of the spiritual gifts that God set in the church that is mentioned in 1 Corinthians 12:10 and so is divers kinds of tongues and interpretation.

In Chapter 14, Paul teaches mostly on prophecy, tongues, and interpretation in a church setting and about edifying the church. Paul then tells us why it would be more beneficial in a church setting to prophesy rather than speak with tongues, unless there is an interpretation.

1 Corinthians 14:2-5

> *² For he that speaketh in an unknown tongue speaketh not unto men, but unto God: for no man understandeth him; howbeit in the spirit he speaketh mysteries.*
>
> *³ But he that prophesieth speaketh unto men to edification, and exhortation, and comfort.*
>
> *⁴ He that speaketh in an unknown tongue edifieth himself; but he that prophesieth edifieth the church.*
>
> *⁵ I would that ye all spake with tongues but rather that ye prophesied: for greater is he that prophesieth than he that speaketh with tongues, except he interpret, that the church may receive edifying.*

Prophecy is divinely inspired utterance given by the Holy Spirit and spoken in one's known language.

1 Corinthians 14: 12-19

> *¹² Even so ye, forasmuch as ye are zealous of spiritual gifts, seek that ye may excel to the edifying of the church.*

135

¹³ Wherefore let him that speaketh in an unknown tongue pray that he may interpret.

¹⁴ For if I pray in an unknown tongue, my spirit prayeth, but my understanding is unfruitful.

¹⁵ What is it then? <u>I will pray with the spirit, and I will pray with the understanding also: I will sing with the spirit, and I will sing with the understanding also.</u>

¹⁶ Else when thou shalt bless with the spirit, how shall he that occupieth the room of the unlearned say Amen at thy giving of thanks, seeing he understandeth not what thou sayest?

¹⁷ <u>For thou verily gives thanks well, but the other is not edified.</u>

¹⁸ I thank my God, I speak with tongues more than ye all:

¹⁹ <u>Yet in the church I had rather speak five words with my understanding,</u> that by my voice <u>I might teach others</u> also, than ten thousand words in an unknown tongue.

Here the Apostle Paul is speaking of when he is preaching or teaching a sermon in a church setting. Why would he tell the church to desire spiritual gifts if we should not or could not have them?

Let's continue with 1 Corinthians 14:26

How is it then, brethren? when ye come together [in a church service], every one of you hath a psalm [spiritual song], hath a doctrine [teaching], hath a tongue, hath a revelation [disclosure of special knowledge], hath an interpretation. Let all things be done unto edifying.

So, we can see in the early church there was no lack of tongues nor lack of spiritual gifts, but rather an abundance of them.

Continuing in 1 Corinthians 14:27-32

²⁷ If any man speak in an unknown tongue, let it be by two, or at the most by three, and that by course; and let one interpret.

²⁸ But if there be no interpreter, let him keep silence in the church; and let him speak to himself, and to God.

²⁹ Let the prophets speak two or three, and let the other judge.

30 If any thing be revealed to another that sitteth by, let the first hold his peace.

31 <u>For ye may all prophesy one by one</u>, that all may learn, and all may be comforted.

32 And the spirits of the prophets are subject to the prophets.

Again, this is speaking of tongues in a church setting. When tongues are given publicly to the congregation, they should be interpreted.

In this chapter, we have looked at the gifts of the Spirit that God set in the church. I encourage you to look up, study and mediate on the following scriptures which further show the workings of the Holy Spirit throughout the Church Age.

- Romans 5:5; 8:1-16, 26, 27; 14:17
- 1 Corinthians 2:4, 5; 10:12, 13, 14
- 2 Corinthians 3:17, 18; 6:16-18; 13:14
- Galatians 3:2, 3; 4:4-6; 5:16, 25
- Ephesians 1:13; 2:18-22; 3:16; 5:18, 19; 6:10, 18
- Philippians 2:1
- 1 Thessalonians 1:5, 6; 4:8; 5:19, 20
- 1 Timothy 4:1
- 2 Timothy 1:14
- Titus 3:5, 6
- Hebrews 2:4; 3:6-8; 10:15
- 1 Peter 1:10-12
- 2 Peter 1:20, 21
- 1 John 3:24; 4:13; 5:7
- Jude 1:17-21

We see the Holy Spirit has been at work throughout the entire Church Age and is mentioned by name in almost every book of the New Testament. Now let's look in the Book of Revelation, which is the last book of the New Testament. We find the Holy Spirit will still be at work throughout the entire Church Age. The Book of Revelation is a letter (Epistle) written to the

Church. The Church is identified in scripture as the born-again ones (all who are saved), which is the church or the body of Christ (John 3:3; John 3:16, 17; Ephesians 1:22, 23; Romans 12:4, 5; Colossians 1:18; Ephesians 5:27, 30; 1 Corinthians 12:12, 13, 27).

Having an ear to hear what the Spirit of God says will ensure our overcoming (1John 2:13, 14; 5:4, 5). Seven times in the first three chapters of the Book of Revelation, Jesus instructs us to have an ear to hear what the Holy Spirit is saying to the churches. Each of the seven references is preceded by or followed by a promise to the overcomer. The first mention is found in Revelation 2:7, where Jesus says, *"He that hath an ear, let him hear what the Spirit saith unto the churches; To him that overcometh will I give to eat of the tree of life, which is in the midst of the paradise of God."* The other six references in Revelation are 2:11, 17, 29; 3:5, 6, 12, 13, 21, 22.

Then we see in the last chapter of Revelation, the Holy Spirit and the Church, called the Bride of Christ, working together and saying...

Revelation 22:17, 20

> *17 And the Spirit and the bride [the Church] say, Come. And let him that heareth say, Come. And let him that is athirst come. And whosoever will, let him take the water of life freely.*
>
> *20 He which testifieth these things saith, Surely I come quickly. Amen. Even so, come, Lord Jesus.*

In the final chapter on the Holy Spirit, we will see some of the workings of the Holy Ghost in believers' lives.

Chapter 21

Holy Spirit's Work in the Christian's Life

(Benefits of Being Baptized with the Holy Spirit)

It is important to know how the Holy Spirit works in a Christian's life, so I have included in this chapter some of the workings that have brought many victories in my life.

There is no salvation without the Spirit of God's involvement. There are no miracles, no revelation, no guidance from God without the Spirit of God. The Holy Spirit is also the revealer of the deep things of God (1 Corinthians 2:10). If you do not allow the Holy Spirit and God's Word to influence your life and guide you, you will be influenced and guided by people, circumstances and even other spirits.

The promise given by God and spoken through the prophets in the Old Testament declared that the Holy Spirit would come to infill and empower believers (Joel 2:28-32), to enable believers to do the works of God. The infilling (baptism) of the Holy Spirit is a promise made to the church for the entire church age.

Every born again one, regardless of denomination, is part of the body of Christ (the church) and God is now their heavenly Father. And as our Heavenly Father, He has a gift for His children. This promised gift is found in Luke 11:13, *"If ye then, being evil [earthly], know how to give good gifts unto your children: how much more shall your heavenly Father <u>give the Holy Spirit</u> to* *them that ask him?"*

So, we can see we need this gift. You can live a powerless life by going through the motions and following doctrines of men, or you can be filled (baptized) with the Holy Spirit of God and live a power-filled life

There are three encounters every believer should have with the Holy Spirit.

1. Being born again of the Spirit (John 3:5).

2. Being baptized in the Spirit (Acts 1:4, 5).

3. Being led by the Spirit (Romans 8:14).

Jesus Himself said we should be filled with the Holy Spirit.

John 7:37-39

> *37 In the last day, that great day of the feast, Jesus stood and cried, saying, If any man thirst, let him come unto me, and drink.*
>
> *38 He that believeth on me, as the scripture hath said, out of his belly shall flow rivers of living water.*
>
> *39 (But this spake he of the Spirit, which they that believe on him should receive: for the Holy Ghost was not yet given; because that Jesus was not yet glorified.)*

We're told to be filled with the Spirit (Ephesians 5:18), and we are instructed to pray in the Spirit (Romans 8:26, 27; Ephesians 6:18). We are to build ourselves up by praying in the Holy Ghost (Jude 1:20). We're told to walk in the Spirit (Galatians 5:16, 25).

Why?

Because the natural man cannot understand the Word of God, the unrenewed mind will reason you out of the things of God. It goes with the wisdom of this world. It sides in with the sense realm. Its logic is based on human reasoning and not on the Word of God, which lives and abides forever. 1 Corinthians 2:14 says, *"But the natural man receiveth not the things of the Spirit of God: for they are foolishness unto him: neither can he know them, because they are spiritually discerned."* See Romans 8:5-8 for more understanding.

It is the Holy Spirit Who gives us revelation of the things of God.

1 Corinthians 2:10, 12

> *¹⁰ But God hath revealed them unto us by his Spirit: for the Spirit sear-cheth all things, yea, the deep things of God.*

> *¹² Now we have received, not the spirit of the world, but the spirit which is of God; that we might know the things that are freely given to us of God.*

We are told the Holy Spirit will live in us.

1 Corinthians 3:16 *"Know ye not that ye are the temple of God, and that the Spirit of God dwelleth in you?*

1 Corinthians 6:19, 20

> *¹⁹ What? know ye not that your body is the temple of the Holy Ghost which is in you, which ye have of God, and ye are not your own?*

> *²⁰ For ye are bought with a price: therefore glorify God in your body, and in your spirit, which are God's.*

Here are some of the workings of the Holy Spirit in a believer's life. I have included scripture references for each one, and I encourage you to look them up and study them for yourself. I know if you will do this, they will be a great blessing to you.

- He will dwell in you (John 14:17).
- He will manifest the things of Christ to those who keep God's Word (John 14:21).
- He will teach you (John 14:26).
- He will testify of Jesus (John 15:26).
- He will guide you into all truth (John 16:13).
- He will glorify Jesus and will show you things to come (John 16:14).
- He will empower and enable you to do what God has called you to do (Acts 1:8).
- He is the Spirit of Life (Romans 8:2). It says in Romans 8:9, *"If any man does not have the Spirit of Christ, he is none of His."*

- He will quicken your mortal body (Romans 8:11).

- He will lead you. Romans 8:14 says, *"For as many as are led by the Spirit of God, they are the sons of God."*

- He will bear witness with your spirit that you are a child of God (Romans 8:16, 1 John 5:10).

- He will help you pray out things for which you don't know how to pray (Romans 8:26, 27; 1 Corinthians 14:14, 15).

- No man can say that Jesus is Lord, but by the Holy Ghost (1 Corinthians 12:3).

- You can pray and sing in the Spirit (1 Corinthians 14:14, 15).

We are not to grieve the Holy Spirit of God, whereby we are sealed unto the day of redemption (Ephesians 1:13, 4:30). We are not to quench the Spirit nor despise prophesying (1 Thessalonians 5:19, 20).

It's by the Holy Spirit that you know you are in Jesus Christ, God's Son (1 John 3:23, 24; 1 John 4:13).

The greatest thing that ever happened to me in my life was when I was born again and passed from spiritual death into eternal life. The second greatest thing was when I was baptized in the Holy Spirit. As I have said earlier in this book, I received Christ as my Savior at age 11. And I was 13 when I received the Holy Spirit baptism with the evidence of speaking in other tongues, just as they did in the Book of Acts. However, I wasn't taught that I should continue to yield to the Holy Spirit in my prayer and worship time. Since at that time I did not personally know the scriptures on this matter, I very seldom spoke or prayed in tongues as God's Word instructs us to do (Romans 8:26, 27; 1 Corinthians 14:14, 15). It was only after I learned more about the works of the Holy Spirit and seeing I could fellowship with Him that I began to be led by the Spirit, and I continue to enjoy fellowship with Him to this day.

As I have studied the scriptures and meditated on them, they have blessed my life and often encouraged me to know that the same Spirit that raised Christ from the dead is the same Spirit that is now quickening, administering life and healing my mortal body (Romans 8:11). This same Spirit now lives in me, guides me, enables me to be and do all I have been called to do as one of Christ's followers and as a part of His body, the church. John 14:15-26 says this same Spirit will be our Comforter and will be with us forever.

I often reflect on the eternal truth Zechariah spoke in the Old Testament.

Zechariah 4:6 *"Then he answered and spake unto me, saying, This is the word of the Lord unto Zerubbabel, saying, <u>Not by might, nor by power, but by my spirit</u>, saith the Lord of hosts."*

This was so important to me because I now realized that it doesn't depend upon my natural ability, but I can depend on His supernatural ability which comes from my Helper, the Holy Spirit.

Let's look at more benefits of being baptized in the Spirit and praying in tongues. God gives you a heavenly language when you are baptized in the Holy Spirit so that now you can pray out the plan of God for yourself as well as the plan of God in the earth. God wants us, His Spirit-filled children, praying in the Spirit. We can pray out mysteries. We can pray out hidden things. We can pray out the will of God when we don't know what to pray or how to pray about a matter by allowing the Holy Spirit Himself to pray through us (Romans 8:26, 27).

The Apostle Paul knew the value of praying in the Holy Spirit.

- In 1 Corinthians 14:2 he says we pray out mysteries.
- In 1 Corinthians 14:4 he says the one praying in the Spirit edifies himself.

Like the Apostle Paul, once we receive the Holy Spirit, we believers can now pray in the Spirit. 1 Corinthians 14:15, *"What is it then? I will pray with the spirit, and I will pray with the understanding also: I will sing with the spirit, and I will sing with the understanding also."*

Ephesians 6:18 tells us to pray always in the Spirit. We are told that we build ourselves up on our most holy faith praying in the Holy Ghost (Jude 1:20).

Jesus says in John 14:20, *"At that day [when the Holy Spirit has come to dwell in you] you will know that I am in the Father and you are in me and I am in you."* When I came to an understanding of what Jesus was telling me here, I then knew that by the Word of God and by the Spirit of God that God, the Father, God, the Son, and God, the Holy Ghost, are dwelling in me, and I am never alone. I declare this great truth with my lips almost every day, giving thanks for their presence with me and in me. I now know what the Apostle John was telling us in 1 John 4:4, *"Greater is He that is in you than he that is in the world."* This is a truth we should never forget.

The One in us is greater than any sickness or disease, and greater than the work of the curse.

God wants you and I as children of God to know that the greater One is in us, and it's the Holy Spirit that leads us into all truth. The One (Jesus) who defeated Satan and redeemed us is in us. The One in us is greater than any sickness or disease, and greater than the work of the curse (Deuteronomy 28). The work Jesus Christ did on the cross is far greater than any devil or demon that could be arrayed against us. He is greater than any attack the enemy might bring. The One in us is greater.

The Holy Ghost is so necessary in our lives for a life of victory. The greatest favor we will ever do ourselves is to learn the truths of God's Word and walk in them with the guidance of the Holy Spirit.

John 8:31, 32

> *31 Then said Jesus to those Jews which believed on him, <u>If ye continue in my word</u>, then are ye my disciples indeed;*
>
> *32 And <u>ye shall know the truth, and the truth shall make you free</u>.*

If we want to receive the promises of God, we must know and believe the Word of God. It is so important that we build our lives on the Word and not upon traditions of men or denominational doctrines. If we do not personally know what the Word has to say about a matter, it is possible to exalt our traditions above the Word of God. This can also happen by not having knowledge of the Holy Spirit.

Once the Holy Spirit was poured out on the day of Pentecost, He has continued His work in the lives of believers throughout the entire New Testament, even to the very last chapter in the Bible, the Book of Revelation.

The Holy Spirit is here to encourage us. I remember a time when I was teaching a weekly Bible study that had stopped for spring break. I wasn't studying and praying as much as I normally would during the break because I was looking for a chair I wanted to purchase for my house. On that Thursday afternoon, I was in my kitchen washing dishes when it felt like a dark blanket of discouragement dropped on me and these thoughts came to me, "You are never going to do the things prophesied about you!" At first, I entertained these thoughts, but then I caught myself realizing these thoughts were from the enemy, the devil; and so, I said within myself, "Hey, I know who this is, and I am not going to listen to you." Then I started praising the Lord for all He had done for me, including raising me up from a bed of sickness. And then I said to the Lord, "I know you have been faithful to me and you will do all that you said you would do." I began to praise Him for the things that He had already done and for the things He was allowing me to do in the kingdom of God. Then I began to praise Him in tongues to which the Holy Spirit gave me the interpretation. In my Bible study, I had been teaching on how the children of Israel had failed to enter the promised land because of unbelief (Numbers 13), and this is what the Holy Spirit gave me that Thursday afternoon to encourage me.

How to Possess Your Possessions

When I called my people out
from a land of bondage and of woe.
I gave them a land, a bountiful land
into which <u>they all could go</u>.

With a strong arm, I led them out.
With signs and wonders to see.
When they came to the land, they searched it
and found it all I said it would be.

When the ten gave report on the land,
they said, "Things contrary seem to be
of our entering in and possessing the land
for there are giants in the land, you see."

Now, if you enter into this land,
it will be only by me.
If you enter in, yes, if you enter in,
<u>My Word you must believe.</u>

If you put your trust in the word of men

who speak contrary to me,
you will not enter in, you will not enter in
to the <u>Provisions I have made</u> for thee.

But two said, "No! Into this land we can go.
For the Lord has given it unto thee.
Only do not doubt; it will keep you out.
Fear not! For the Lord will fight for thee!"

Do not hearken to the men in the land
who would presume to speak against me.
For their words shall fall, but my Words
shall stand through all eternity!

And still today if you will enter in
to the promises I have given to thee,
you must look by faith to the Word of God
for this is the entrance for thee.

My sheep hear my voice.
They hear, and they follow me.
And how shall they hear?
Oh, how shall they hear?
Through my Word I have given to thee.

Yes, and still today, if you would enter in
to the promises I have given to thee,
you must walk by Faith in My Living Word.
For if you walk by sight, you may long to go in,
but only the giants you will see.

In all my Bible studies, I encourage those attending to study and memorize Colossians 1:9-14 until it becomes reality to them. One day when I was sitting and meditating on these verses, God gave me these words in English.

New Kingdom

I'm in a new kingdom.
I serve a new Lord.
I have a new Master,
and He is good.

I am an heir of redemption.
Ransom in full.
I now have access to
Christ's total work.

There is safety; there is refuge;
there is deliverance from all
of sin's dreaded payday
that came through man's fall.

There is healing; there
is wholeness; there is peace; there is joy.
I am invited by my Father
to partake of it all.

At one time when I was praising the Lord because I was so thankful that I had learned how to recognize the work of the enemy (John 10:10) and that I had been redeemed from the curse and made an heir of all the blessings of the work of Christ on the cross, the Holy Spirit gave me the following.

Refuse Sickness and Disease

I refuse sickness and disease
in Jesus' Holy name.
For Jesus set me free;
oh, that is why He came.
To open prison doors;
to set the captives free.
To bear our sin and shame;
to ransom you and me.
Upon His precious back,
the stripes there were laid.
He was our substitute;
the price He has paid.
The work He did that day
was for all eternity.
Whoever will may come,
and receive abundantly.
Of principalities and powers,
He made an open show.

Triumphing over them;
victorious He arose.
Yes, Jesus is my Lord;
He gained the victory.
And all He did that day,
He did for you and me.
So rise up in Jesus' name,
and walk free from that place.
Of sickness and disease,
for Jesus took your place.
The doors are open now;
rise up in Jesus' name.
Walk free from that place;
your freedom Jesus gained.

These are just a few examples of how the Holy Ghost has worked in my life. There is a testimony I would like to share with you about how mightily the Holy Ghost worked in the life of a man named Alton. This is one of the most amazing testimonies of the importance of learning to measure and know where your thoughts come from; and how learning this brought victory into Alton's life.

I grew up on one of the mountains in Alabama. This is where I came to know Alton. Alton was married to Juanita, whose family was a nearby neighbor of ours when I was growing up. Juanita knew about my miracle and how the Lord had raised me up and healed me when I was a semi-invalid.

One year when I was up on the mountain attending a meeting, both Alton and Juanita were there. We were all gathered in the overflow room in the church having a meal when I first saw Alton. He was sitting there just like a zombie. Later, when I passed by them, Juanita said, "Opal, I want you to pray for Alton." So, I reached out my hand, laid it on him, and prayed for him. After the dinner, we then went to the sanctuary for a singing. It was there the Holy Spirit prompted me to go over and sit by Alton so I could give him scriptures, explain them to him and tell him to read them daily.

I obeyed the Holy Ghost and went over and sat next to him. I shared with him how, just before I had received my victory of healing, the enemy came. I told him about the morning when I was hurting so badly that I asked my son to anoint me with oil and pray for me. After my son had done this, no sooner had he gotten out the front door that the enemy's thoughts came and said to me, "You have misused the oil!" At this time, I didn't know how to recognize the enemy's thoughts. I didn't know that it was his thought. And he made it sound like I had committed an unpardonable sin by misusing the oil and so, I started repenting.

When the enemy saw that I didn't recognize it was him or that it was his thought, he started coming with all kinds of thoughts, wicked and unholy thoughts. I would plead the blood of Jesus and ask forgiveness for those thoughts. And then I would tell the Lord, "Lord, I would rather please you than to breathe another breath. I would rather please you than to live another day. I would rather please you than to have all the wealth of the world." And I meant it, and He knew I meant it.

Every time I would start to pray, the enemy would come with those same unholy and wicked thoughts. He would say, "You couldn't think a thought like that and be a Christian. You're not healed, and you're not going to get healed." And then he said, "You're not even going to go to heaven when you die." This attack continued for two weeks. Then early one morning, the Holy Spirit opened up the scripture Hebrews 4:12 to me which says:

> *For the word of God is quick, and powerful, and sharper than any two-edged sword, piercing even to the <u>dividing asunder of soul and spirit</u>, and of the joints and marrow, and is a <u>discerner of the thoughts and intents of the heart</u>.*

The Holy Spirit pointed out to me that this scripture says it <u>divides between the spirit and the soul</u>. I didn't know at that time there was a difference between the spirit and the soul; that we are a spirit being, we have a soul, and we live in a body. We can easily see the body and know what the body is. But it was important for me to learn the difference between the spirit and the soulish area; and that it's the spirit that gets born again. Your soul is your mind, will, and emotions; the decision-making part of you. It did not get born again and so we must do something about that part of us. We must renew our mind with the Word of God (James 1:21, Romans 12:1, 2).

And so, when the Holy Spirit opened this scripture up to me, He showed me that God looks on the heart (spirit), and God knew what was in my heart. God looks at the intents of the heart as the scripture says, and God knew I wanted to please Him; and so, God let me know who it was bringing those thoughts. And so, when I started praying early that morning, here came the enemy with all those thoughts. I just stopped and said, "Alright devil. I recognize you, and those are not my thoughts. They're your thoughts. And I rebuke you in the name of Jesus." And I went on and reminded him of what Jesus had done to him for me and for the world. I reminded him that he's going to the pit and then he will be cast into the lake of fire where he'll burn forever and ever. Well, hearing talk like that, he didn't stay around. He fled and took his thoughts with him. And he didn't come and try that too many more times, but every time he did come I would stop and rebuke him, and he would flee. I overcame him as the Bible tells us to do in Revelation 12:11. Every time the devil comes, we must fight with the Word of God and overcome him.

"Alright devil. I recognize you, and those are not my thoughts. They're your thoughts. And I rebuke you in the name of Jesus."

And so, I explained all this to Alton and gave him the understanding of this scripture the Holy Spirit had given to me. That's when I saw the first spark of life in Alton who said, "That was the devil telling me I wanted to kill myself, wasn't it?" I said, "Well, it sure was." Alton had not recognized that these thoughts were from a suicide spirit. And so, I had his wife write the scriptures down which included Revelation 12:11, Hebrews 4:12, Colossians 1:9-14 as well as others. I knew Alton was born again, but he didn't understand where those thoughts were coming from and he didn't understand how to fight. But now, Alton knew what was happening to him and where those thoughts had been coming from; and he had the scriptures I had given to him to read daily.

When I saw Alton a couple months later in a meeting which I had invited him and his wife to attend, he was just sitting in the service so happy with a smile on his face. The following year when I saw him on the mountain, he said to me, "I'm still reading those scriptures every day, and I'm just enjoying living. Life is normal again." Later I asked Juanita how long Alton had been in that condition, and she said it had been about 4 years. Again, it is so important to know the enemy's works in order to measure your thoughts with the Word of God so that you will not entertain his thoughts but cast them down as we are told to do in the Bible.

2 Corinthians 10:3-5

³ For though we walk in the flesh, we do not war after the flesh:

⁴ (For the weapons of our warfare are not carnal, but mighty through God to the pulling down of strong holds;)

⁵ Casting down imaginations, and every high thing that exalteth itself against the knowledge of God, and bringing into captivity every thought to the obedience of Christ.

This is one of the scriptures the Holy Spirit taught me that has brought many victories into my life, and to many with whom I have shared it, and that is to learn to measure each thought by the Word of God. Is the thought from the kingdom of God or from your enemy Satan? We would not be instructed to do this if the enemy could not bring thoughts to our mind from the kingdom of darkness…doubt thoughts, unbelief thoughts, worry thoughts, discouraging thoughts, and lies of Satan are all from the kingdom of darkness from which you have been delivered. Take every contrary thought captive that doesn't measure up with the Word of God. This is how we win in every spiritual battle.

Many people have gotten discouraged and given up their walk with God because they didn't recognize the thoughts coming to them were not theirs but were from the enemy, the devil. During your walk with the Lord, the enemy will try to get you to give up. It is so important to learn how to measure every thought by the Word of God.

The Lord tells us in Isaiah 26:3, *"Thou wilt keep him in perfect peace, whose mind is stayed on thee: because he trusteth in thee."* The Holy Spirit is here to guide us and empower us to overcome every attack the enemy, Satan, brings.

The baptism of the Holy Spirit is God's gift for His children (Luke 11:11-13) and is a work of the same Holy Spirit that performed the new birth in you. It is an infilling and an overflowing of the Holy Spirit of God in you. If you have been born again but have not yet received the baptism of the Holy Spirit which God has promised, I encourage you to receive Him now. To receive this gift, just say from your heart, "Lord, I ask you for the gift of the Holy Ghost." Now, open your mouth, yield yourself to the Spirit of God and begin to speak out the sounds or utterances that rise up from your innermost being. Yield your vocal chords to speak out the utterances the Holy Spirit of God gives you as in Acts 2:4, *"And they were all filled with the Holy Ghost, and began to speak with other tongues, as the Spirit gave them utterance."* When the Holy Spirit gives the utterance, you must give voice to it and speak it out with your tongue. The Holy Ghost is a gift promised by Jesus. Receive it as yours.

Some have longed to be filled and speak in other tongues, but they are waiting for the Holy Spirit to make them speak. The Holy Spirit never makes anyone speak or pray even in their known language; He only urges or prompts you to do so. The same is true with praying in the Spirit. Remember, Paul said after he was filled with the Holy Spirit, *"I will pray with the Spirit, and I will pray with the understanding also."* It was many years later after being baptized in the Holy Spirit that I learned that I could and should pray in the Spirit. And doing this has brought many victories into my life. By praying things out in the Spirit, many times God has shown me things to come and the outcome/answer to the problem/need (John 16:13).

As you diligently study the Word, you will find many more things the Holy Spirit has come to do in the believer's life that are too numerous to include in this book. But as you study them and get to know your Guide, the Holy Spirit, better, you will grow spiritually and live out the victories that God, through His Son, Jesus Christ, has made available to you.

Chapter 22

Testimonies

Ray Hall (Opal's younger brother) Testimonies:

Testimony #1: I would like to share with you a special need that God met in my life. In the summer of 1972, my wife Sue and I had been married seven years and were unable to have children. We had applied for adoption and were close to receiving our child when our plans changed. We were visiting my sisters, Aleene and Irene, and Opal's spiritual mother, Sister Beatrice Stansky, was there as well. When we came together for a time of prayer, Sister Stansky prayed for Sue and by the Holy Spirit, told her that God was giving her the desires of her heart. Sue and I both took this to mean that God was giving us a child. We knew that God still keeps the promise He gave in Psalm 113:9, *"He maketh the barren woman to keep house, and to be a joyful mother of children. Praise ye the LORD."* and so we stood on this scripture until this Word was performed in us. Less than one year later, my wife gave birth to a handsome baby boy that we named Christopher Ray; and then two and a half years later, God gave Christopher a little sister whom we named Susan Renee', and now together they have given us six lovely and lively grandchildren! Praise God!

Testimony #2: In the early 1980's I began having migraine headaches which would typically occur on a Saturday. They were totally debilitating and were always accompanied by an upset stomach. Medication didn't help. All I could do was get in a dark room, put an ice pack on my face and let the headache run its course. Because the headaches would only occur about twice a month, it was something I thought I could manage, and so I just accepted it as a fact of life for several years. In the mid-1980's my wife and I went to Birmingham with Opal and her husband, Don, to attend some services that Reverend Kenneth Hagin, Sr. was conducting at one of the local churches. The first service was on a Saturday night, and I hadn't come to the service for healing. That night Reverend Hagin spoke on "Healing is the Children's Bread" and that every Christian should be convinced of the fact that God has prepared a table for us, His children, but we each must come to the table and partake of His healing bread. This message brought conviction to my heart that I, a born-again child of God, filled with the Spirit, had put up with those head-aches for way too long and had never sought God's healing. I determined then that at the first opportunity I had I would ask for prayer for healing from the migraine headaches. We came back to the Sunday morning service. I don't really remember the sermon that morning, but at the conclusion of the service, an opportunity was given for those needing healing to come forward for prayer. I remember I was a little disappointed when Reverend Hagin said, "I'm not going to pray for the sick this morning; instead I'm going to ask one of my worship leaders to pray." So, this young lady prayed for me, and I was gloriously touched, slain in the Spirit, and received my healing from migraine headaches; and I have never had another one since. Opal found out later that this young lady who had prayed for me was Anne Durant. Praise God!

Testimony #3: In the early 1990's I started having severe problems with my back. I developed a pain in my lower left back that ran down my left leg. The pain seemed almost constant but more intense at certain times. I was anointed and prayed for several times, but I couldn't seem to have the faith I needed to receive my healing. I had received a physical manifestation (slain in the Spirit) when I was healed of migraine headaches, and I guess I was expecting a similar manifestation with healing for my back; and since the symptoms were more or less constant, I was probably guilty of looking at the symptoms more than the promises of God. In short, God needed to grow my faith before I received my healing for my back. My sister, Opal, felt led to give me the book, *Christ the Healer* by F. F. Bosworth. My wife and I took a trip to the Gulf Coast shortly after this and during this time I read and reread this book and also studied the scriptures that were referenced in the book. God used the sermons in *Christ the Healer* to build my faith in His promises of healing and to more clearly show me what <u>my part</u> was in His healing process. I learned that all of God's salvation, including healing for the body, is "by grace through faith" and that we have a part in this process. Our part, when we pray or when we are prayed for, is to believe that we receive. After continuing to study the messages in *Christ the Healer* and planting the Word of God that Reverend Bosworth referenced in his sermons in my heart, I was ready to reap the harvest of healing for my back; so while praying alone at home, my healing manifested. All praise and glory to Christ the Healer!

Summation:

We have a common enemy whom Jesus describes as a lying thief who comes to steal, kill, and destroy. With every healing manifested in my life, the thief came again with symptoms trying to get me to walk by sight and feeling and to doubt that I had really received my healing. So, be prepared when the enemy comes, to meet him with "It is written," "It is written," "It is written" as our Lord Jesus taught us. Our faith cannot stand on physical improvements. It must stand totally on God's Word which is our rock and our solid foundation. All other ground is sinking sand. In fact, when symptoms would try to reoccur, I would sing the song, "The Healer." The chorus is taken from Isaiah 53:5, *"He was wounded for our transgressions, he was bruised for our iniquities. Surely, He bore all our sorrows, and by His stripes, we are healed."*

Jesus hasn't changed. He's still the Savior and He's still the Healer. He is the way, the truth, and the life. He is God's only salvation. He is the Author and Finisher of our faith. He is our soon coming King. Praise His name forever more.

Reference:

Opal and I both recommend the book *Christ The Healer* by F. F. Bosworth on the subject of divine healing. Reverend Bosworth had a very successful healing ministry during the early twentieth century. The book contains fourteen excellent sermons on faith and healing, and many testimonies of people who either received their healing in his services or by reading this book. This book is for anyone who needs help in building their faith in the area of divine healing. This book can be obtained on the Internet. Just Google Christ the Healer PDF; one of the first links to appear will be "HOPEFAITHPRAYER. COM" You can click this link and read *Christ the Healer* online by clicking preview or download the book for free. You can also find an audible reading of each of the sermons on YouTube.

Glenda D. Testimony:

Some years ago, my doctor told me I needed a liver transplant. After the diagnosis, I was invited to Healing School taught by Miss Opal Crews. This was six weeks before I was scheduled for three days of testing before going on the transplant list. When I started hearing the Word of God about healing, my heart soaked it in and it gave me the faith to receive my provision of healing for my liver. I went for the three days of testing, and the doctors saw that everything was improving and sent me home. I had to go back periodically for testing; finally, the doctors told me that my liver was now as good as anyone else's in the room. I never needed a liver transplant because I was healed by the Word of God. I continue to hear and receive His Word today so I can walk in the healing power of God. Praise the Lord!

Testimonies received during the ministry of Opal Crews:

Buddy Medley healed of staph infection: Buddy attended a class I taught on healing for six weeks at my former church. At the end of the last class, the Holy Spirit prompted me to give those attending an opportunity to act on what they had heard. The first one up for prayer was Buddy who had recently started coming to the church. Buddy said that for the last four years he had been dealing with a staph infection which had caused him to break out in boils that would need to be lanced and drained. In fact, he had a boil on his body that day that he didn't mention. This infection would require him to wash his clothes in a special solution. He said he was taking antibiotics, each one stronger than the other, but none got rid of the infection. I was then prompted to ask him, "Are you ready to get rid of it?" He said, "Yes I am." So, I prayed for him, and at the end of prayer he left and headed to the service. I found out later that after the service, as he walked down a long flight of stairs to leave the building, he felt the boil disappear. He wanted to look and see that it was gone, but he said Miss Opal had taught him that we don't look to see, but we look at the Word of God. He was cured of the staph infection, and it never returned again. Praise God!

Sister Franklin healed in a home meeting: After I had received my own healing, my friend Grace, who lived in Tennessee, wanted me to come see her. I still had symptoms in my body and couldn't drive that distance, so I flew. The Lord let me know that while I was in Tennessee, Sister Stansky would have a place lined up for me to speak. It turned out to be a meeting in my friend's home. Sister Franklin, who was from Grace's church attended the home meeting. She had not been able to lift either of her arms for about two years. I shared my testimony on how the Lord had healed me and raised me up. Then, at the end, I prayed for those wanting prayer. Sister Franklin was one of those that came up for prayer. The next morning Sister Franklin called Grace and told her that she was totally healed. She said, "It's so wonderful to be free of pain and that she could fix her own hair that morning." Through the weeks and months that followed, she would continue to tell Grace "It's so good to be free of pain." Hallelujah!

Brother Andrews healed in Trinidad: One year later after the Lord had healed me, I went on my first mission trip to Trinidad (West Indies) with Sister Stansky. I stayed with one of the church ladies, Pat, whose husband was a builder. Mr. Andrews, who kept their books, came to their house that day to work on them. Pat told him we were there conducting services in the churches and that I was there to give my testimony of healing. Mr. Andrews said he would like to hear about healing because one of his arms was locked in position. Pat came to the kitchen where I was sitting at the table talking with her husband and some of his friends about the Lord and said, "Mr. Andrews wants you to come and tell him about healing." So, I went to the living room where he was and taught him that we receive healing by faith just as we receive Jesus as our Savior by faith. He said "Faith! I heard someone mention that word on the radio last week." I thought, "Oh me, he doesn't know a thing about faith!" So, I gave him several books on healing, faith and on the Holy Spirit. I told him we would be in his area in another two weeks and told him to come to the meeting and I would pray for him then. The Holy Spirit spoke to my heart and said, "You pray for him now. He might not get to come to that meeting." So, I said, "OK Lord." I went and got the lady evangelist who was traveling with us. Then I taught him further on healing and told him that Jesus said in Mark 11:24 what things soever you desire when you pray, believe that you receive them, and you shall have them. I said, "Are you ready to do that? Believe you receive when we pray?" He said, "Yes." I asked him twice, and his answer was the same, so I laid my hands on him and prayed for his healing in the name of Jesus. Then I told him to lift up that arm and start praising the Lord. He shot his arm up and started walking around the room praising the Lord. He was healed!

Lady healed in Trinidad: I was speaking and sharing my testimony on healing at one of the church services, and at the end of the service I gave everyone an opportunity to come up for prayer. There were so many that came up, that Sister Stansky said to me, and the lady evangelist traveling with us, that we would each take a line of people and pray. A lady with a massive growth on her left breast came up to me for prayer, and after she told me why she had come, I asked her, "Are you ready to receive your healing now?" She answered, "Yes." Then I asked, "Will you receive it when we pray?" She said, "Yes" very firmly, so I laid my hand on her and prayed. I felt that growth diminish in size. She was rejoicing at the end of the prayer. When the lady came back the next night for service, the growth was totally gone. She was healed! It is so important that we have a time when we accept His healing as our own.

Trinidad service healings: At another meeting at the same church, I invited people to come up for prayer. After prayer, there were seven to eight men who stood and testified they had received their healing that night.

Janice W. healed during an Aglow meeting: I was ministering at an Aglow meeting (international ladies group), and I shared my testimony that night of how I had taken my healing by faith in the Word and walked it out over some time. Janice, who was the Vice President of one of the local chapters, attended the meeting. At the close of the meeting, I invited people to come up for prayer. Janice came and said she had been having a back problem for several years and had been prayed for many times; but during the service, while she heard the Word, she now knew how to receive her healing and had claimed her healing. I asked her, "What could you not do before?" She said, "I could not mop my floors." I said, "Pick up a pretend mop and start mopping." She moved in a mopping motion and could do it easily. The Word of God taught her how to receive, and she was healed!

Raymond P. arm healed: While attending a camp meeting in Tulsa, OK, I met a lady named Shirley, who was the Praise and Worship leader at her church in Memphis, TN. She asked if I would come and do some services at her church if she could work it out with her Pastor? I said I would. She called me 2 weeks later and said her Pastor wanted me to come. Although I had said, "Yes," I became apprehensive about going so soon because I didn't know anyone there. The Holy Spirit spoke to me and said, "My Word will thoroughly furnish you and my Spirit will enable you" (2 Timothy 3:16,17). And so, I went and stayed with Shirley and her husband, Raymond, in their home. Raymond was a home builder and was having problems with his arm. It was very painful in the shoulder joint which made it difficult to move. It would hurt so badly some nights he would have to get up, walk the floor and rub his arm. On the morning I was going to share my testimony and pray for the sick, he stayed out of work and came. At the end of the message I gave an opportunity for prayer for those who wanted healing. There was quite a long line, and Raymond was in the back of the line. When he got halfway up, he began to raise his arm and praise the Lord. When he got to me, I said, "Raymond, what did you come for?" He said, "Well, I came to get my healing, but I already got it." He was still praising the Lord because he had received His healing from hearing the Word.

More healed by the Word:

Testimony #1: I was ministering at a church in Illinois on healing; and when I was done, I turned the service back over to the Pastor. The Pastor said to me, "I'm pretty sure there are some that would have liked for you to have prayed for them." But I didn't feel that's the way God wanted it to be done that evening. Before I could respond, a lady attending the service stood up and testified that while I taught, she received her healing for her arm that had been having some numbness and pain. She was healed by hearing the Word, and the Holy Spirit said to me, that's how He wanted to do it that night.

Testimony #2: At another meeting in Illinois, I shared with those attending what the Lord had shown me early in my ministry. I told them God said they would not have to have hands laid on them, but that they would receive by hearing the Word. And when I shared this truth with them in a service, it would happen. A woman with bulging discs and arthritis who had much pain was healed in that morning service. I asked her to come back to the evening service and share her testimony. She did and told the congregation that during the message, a warmth came all over her and the pain left her, and she was healed. Amen!

Testimony #3: When I was ministering in a church in Florida, the associate pastor's wife, who had a large growth on her breast, said the growth had disappeared while I was teaching.

This is just a few of the testimonies. There have been many others who have received their healing.

Prayer for Healing:

Now that you have seen in the scriptures that Jesus Christ took your sins and your diseases at Calvary and you are ready to receive (accept) your healing now, pray this from your heart:

"Lord Jesus, I believe you took all of my sins and all of my diseases when you went to the cross. I come to you now to receive my healing from (name the disease/diseases). I take my healing by faith in your work done for me, and I thank you for performing your healing work in me, and I give you praise. **Amen!**"

Remember that healing is sometimes instantaneous and sometimes it is gradual. But in the process, keep your heart and your mouth in agreement with God's Word.

Please write and share your victory with me so that I may rejoice with you! Please send to:

Opal Crews
Words of Life
PO Box 1985
Huntsville, AL 35807

About the Author

Opal Crews shares her experience of being healed and raised up from a semi-invalid condition of incurable bone and muscle diseases. Knowing God was her only hope, she turned wholeheartedly to the Bible and learned all she could about healing. She learned that healing is not only God's will, but it was provided through the finished work of Jesus Christ. Through faith in His Word, and believing, receiving and walking it out, she was raised up from a semi-invalid condition healed and whole.

God then told her, "You go and speak of My faithfulness to My Word and the work of My Son." This she has been faithful to do. She has taught God's Word in churches throughout the south and in Trinidad and the Philippines. She also teaches God's Word locally through her weekly TV program, "Words of Life." And she teaches a class on healing weekly in her local church. She is also a teacher of the Word in her church's Bible Institute which is used in Bible Institutes in other nations.

Through sharing God's Word, she has seen many encouraged in their walk with the Lord. She has also seen many receive their healing through the laying on of hands and while sitting and hearing God's Word.

All glory to Jesus Christ, our Redeemer and Lord.